"ONE OF THE MOST SOULFUL,
BEAUTIFULLY WRITTEN DOG BOOKS IN RECENT YEARS."
—*USA Today*

"A gem, a small masterpiece . . . *The Rufus Chronicle* appeals not just to dog lovers. It deals with the universal themes of life and death, family, our relationship to nature and our interactions with the other creatures in the world. It's also a book that lovers of good literature and well-worked prose will embrace. Gusewelle's style—simple, direct, concrete, conversational—achieves a high level of artistic excellence, although it never calls attention to itself."

—*Kansas City Star*

"For anyone who has loved, and then lost, a dog, *The Rufus Chronicle* is more heartwarming than heartbreaking—and often very funny as well. . . . Would make a nice gift for anyone who has loved an animal not wisely, but too well."

—*San Antonio Express-News*

"Rarely does a book come along that seems upon first reading like reacquainting oneself with an old friend. . . . *Chronicle* is a time well spent, foraging in the fields of the heart."

—*The Clarion-Ledger* (Jackson, Mississippi)

"This warm and wonderful book not only tells the story of one particularly remarkable dog, Rufus, and the people whose lives he touched so deeply, it also reveals with wit and wisdom the bond that *all* families feel toward their pets. More than that, *The Rufus Chronicle* demonstrates why Charles Gusewelle has been one of the Heartland's best-kept literary secrets—until now."

—DAYTON R. DUNCAN

"Love stories come in many shapes and sizes. Rufus will permeate your heart and invade your soul. What a book, what a dog, what a life. A must-read."

—*Northwest Arkansas Times*

"The book is a delight. . . . I've read more than a few books about men and their dogs, but this one is special and a 'must' for anyone who has owned, trained, hunted [with] and loved their dogs. . . . If you can get through that final chapter without having your eyes mist up a bit, you are made of sterner stuff than I."

—*The Argus Leader* (SD)

D1056180

Books by C. W. Gusewelle

A Paris Notebook

An Africa Notebook

Quick as Shadows Passing

Far From Any Coast

A Great Current Running: The Lena River Expedition

The RUFUS Chronicle
Another Autumn

C. W. Gusewelle

Ballantine Books
New York

Sale of this book without a front cover may be unauthorized. If this book is coverless, it may have been reported to the publisher as "unsold or destroyed" and neither the author nor the publisher may have received payment for it.

A Ballantine Book
Published by The Ballantine Publishing Group

Copyright © 1996 by C. W. Gusewelle

All rights reserved under International and Pan-American Copyright Conventions. Published in the United States by The Ballantine Publishing Group, a division of Random House, Inc., New York, and distributed in Canada by Random House of Canada Limited, Toronto. Originally published by Kansas City Star Books in 1996.

Ballantine and the Ballantine colophon are registered trademarks of Random House, Inc.

www.randomhouse.com/BB/

Library of Congress Catalog Card Number: 99-90621

ISBN: 0-345-42386-0

Cover design by Min Choi
Cover art by Neil Heimsoth

Manufactured in the United States of America

First Ballantine Books Trade Edition: November 1999

10 9 8 7 6 5 4 3 2 1

This book is for Fred Kiewit, Stuart Mitchelson
and Patrick Dolan, who shared many of
Rufus's finest days—and mine.

You walk along the forest edge, you watch your dog,
but all the time images and faces of the beloved,
dead or alive, keep coming to mind ...
All your life unwinds as smoothly and swiftly as a scroll.

Ivan Turgenev
A Sportsman's Notebook

ARCHAEOLOGY

IN SOME FUTURE YEAR, a different proprietor of the land, out walking on a fine spring day, may pass that way—along the abandoned fence row where the blackberry canes are white with bloom and the wild rose makes mounds of pink at the field's edge. That brushy line, in which no posts or wire remain, divides two meadows of native grass that fall away toward the dark of woods on either side.

The walker will discover, tucked in close against a thicket, a curious mound of flat fieldstones, too neatly placed and fitted to be accidental. Curiosity will bring him back there another day, carrying a shovel.

He will lift the stones aside and excavate beneath them, possibly imagining a treasure. But what he will unearth will be only the folded skeleton of a dog, and four large plastic buttons of the kind found on a canvas hunting coat. Also, if he looks carefully, the wing bones—finer than matchsticks—of a small bird.

If that man is a hunter, he will understand immediately what he's found. He will know that the creatures those artifacts represent are gone from there, away to some field of always autumn. I like to think he will replace the earth and stones, and leave the place as it was—a little cache of things that tell no story except when all together—safe again from rushing time.

ONE
1983

MARCH

THE PUPS, EIGHT or 10 of them, were only a few days old—a rubbery tangle of orange and white, eyes not yet open, barely identifiable as dogs. How possibly to choose among them?

We got word of the litter from a friend. They were out of a Brittany owned by his dentist, Joe Gingrich, who had a farm in the Kansas Flint Hills and raised dogs to hunt, not to show. About the sire I knew little except his registry name, Winchester Repeater Seeley.

Gingrich had brought the dam, Rosanna, home to the city to whelp, and she and her pups were nested on a pad of blankets in an alcove just off his kitchen. I liked her looks. She was affectionate with her new brood, nudging them in place with her nose, then arranging herself so they all had a chance, at least, at a faucet.

"Can I give you an assignment?" I asked the dentist's daughter, Jill. At age 12, she'd be sharing the work of caring for the litter.

"You'll see them every day," I said to her. "So I need your help in picking. Keep a lookout for the one that's the most active. The boldest. The one that goes out first from the blanket for adventures on his own."

She seemed pleased by this heavy responsibility.

"Boy or girl?" she asked.

"Boy," I told her.

I live in a household that includes one wife, two daughters and a neutered female beagle-shepherd mix. You get lonely, sometimes, for the company of your own gender.

"What will you call him?"

It is not true that I named him after one of the most prominent bankers in our town. Though if that were so, I would have meant it as a compliment to them both.

"Rufus," I said. It was just a name I liked, though it seemed somehow not quite long enough for a dog of pedigree and noble prospects.

We have a piece of country land two hours from the city—some of it in crops and some left uncleared and unmowed as habitat for wildlife. I remembered, then, from the topographic map, the name that marks the highest point on the farm, where the old house stands. It's Robins Hill, with no apostrophe.

"He'll be Rufus of Robins Hill," I declared importantly. And so he would—though it was uncertain still which one of that puppy tangle he might be.

MAY

MY DAUGHTER, Anne, older by a year than her sister, Jennie, went with me to bring him home. The spring morning was unseasonably raw, so we wrapped him in a blanket with just his head showing for his first journey by car.

We'd gone maybe a dozen blocks when Anne gave a little squeak of surprise.

"He's sprung a leak," she cried.

It was only the first of several notifications that Rufus was not to be, in all ways, a perfect dog.

Bold I'd asked for. Bold we got. A baby's mesh playpen contained him for two days, then he heaved his woolly little self over the top and the kitchen was his. Three days after that he conquered the spring-mounted kitchen door. A day later he solved the stair, extending his territory to the whole of the house.

"Don't worry," I told my wife, Katie. "We're not going to make a pet of him. As soon as he grows a little he'll be an outdoor dog."

The back yard was fenced. A fine new doghouse had been made ready to receive him, its walls insulated and lined with fragrant alfalfa hay. A man can have a true working dog—a bird-finding machine that will smite his hunting chums sullen with envy.

Or he can have an amiable companion, mostly good for petting. One has to choose.

"We already have one indoor dog," I said. That was Cinnamon, rescued from the street and already well on past middle age. "One's plenty."

"And when winter comes?"

"He'll acclimate."

"Right," she said, but she sounded unconvinced.

JULY

So Rufus, or Rufe as we sometimes call him, spends these summer days outdoors. It's not a hard life. He is fed regularly and well, has a large pan of drinking water kept cool and fresh, and a moderate-sized yard to excavate as he pleases, and it pleases him much. He has a couple of nice flower beds to defile.

At night he is allowed to sleep in the bedroom. At first that was only when it rained. Then he began peering through the back door with such an expression of bafflement and desolation that we began letting him in every night, regardless of the weather. We'll have to see how that works out.

He's still just a pup, going on 4 months old but already full of fire and promise—too full of fire to suit the old dog, Cinnamon, who growls at him but does not bite, and whose empty threats have become less credible. He nips at her legs and runs along behind her, her tail in his jaws. He poaches at her food dish and brazenly filches her bones. She looks at us sad-eyed, as if to say: *What's this you've done to me in the ripeness of my years? What does it all mean?*

She cannot remember herself at that age—chewer of shoes, sly defiler of carpets, relentless bedeviler of the cats. Or if she remembers, she does not admit. The years have filled her up: the children's growing, our history in the house, country weekends and delicious wallowings in mud or worse. Short of wind, overtaken by portliness, she had imagined her life as a succession of tranquil days, enlivened only by her once-daily obligation to announce the passage of the postman, Ernie.

Now, horrifically, she finds herself with a family to raise.

It has been a long time—years actually—since I began with a new pup. Other dogs have come to me, half-grown strays or castoffs, and have stayed to be indispensable friends. Two of those, two beagle brothers, stayed 14 years and saw me into marriage and fatherhood.

Rufus is of the pointing spaniel breed. All the tendencies of both the lines seem to have passed to him intact. He already is pointing a quail wing staunchly, stylishly, for as much as a minute, until, in a victory of temptation over will, he gathers himself to pounce and the wing has to be snatched away. When it's gone, he courses over the grass with a fury, hoping to come upon that beguiling scent again.

That is the pointer in his ancestry.

But he also has displayed an early interest in his water pan—not for drinking from, but for climbing into. The first time we took him to the farm, we left him on the pond bank while we went out fishing in the boat. He raced back and forth along the dam, anxious and whining, then flung himself straight in and swam the 50 yards out to us. Now he has a child's wading pool in which he thrashes happily and from which he retrieves thrown balls with unrestrained delight.

That's the spaniel in him.

Where the crocodile got in I can't say. Much of the time he seems all pink mouth and needle teeth. His world is divided into two categories of objects: those made of tempered steel, and thus not edible. And all the rest.

Sometimes, seeing him at play, it is hard to imagine him ever being of any serious use. But then that evening hour comes, when Cinnamon is upstairs asleep and Rufus and I go out for a few purposeful minutes together in the yard. I give him the quail wing to hold before we start, to remind him of the business at hand. In that moment, strangely, the puppy manner leaves him altogether.

He takes the feathered thing gently in his mouth. An expression of great solemnity passes over his face. I think he is in touch then with the sense of what he is and will be. I think he knows the future he contains—of cold mornings and crisp leaves and beddings in the back of cars and the glitter of the birds' eyes in the instant before they burst from the grass.

There are not many things able to tempt a man in middle age to wish the seasons forward, to wish time away. But now, with Rufus, I yearn ahead.

AUGUST

THEY COULD HAVE BEEN brother and sister, so alike they were in size and marking and playful temperament.

"That's a fine-looking pup you have there," I called out to the young couple a little distance across the park.

There's no surer way to friendship than to praise a stranger's dog.

"This is Maggie," the man called back. "And we're

the Maggarts—Dennis and JoAnn."

"My little fellow here is Rufus."

The space between us closed, and after a moment's ceremonial sniffing those two set off to romp and tumble across the grass.

"They make quite a pair," I said.

"Mirror images," agreed Dennis. "Will you hunt him?"

"He was pointing a quail wing at 10 weeks. And Maggie?"

"I'd start her if I had one," he said.

"I think I still have a couple of wings in the freezer," I told him. "If you've got a pencil I'll give you my number. You're welcome to one."

The Maggarts hadn't been married long, and the pretty little Brit was their first dog together. They lived not far from the park.

We loitered awhile, watching the pups play—two merry youngsters, enjoying their freedom but racing back from time to time to check in and get a reassuring pat.

Then we clipped their leashes on.

"You come here often?" Dennis asked.

"Several times a week."

"We're here with Maggie almost every day. We'll look for you and Rufus."

That is how important things sometimes happen,

in an offhand, accidental way. Often after that we were at the park together, watching our lively youngsters grow.

SEPTEMBER

TEAL SEASON IN THE MIDWEST arrives oddly out of time. The days still are warm and the leaves have not yet started to color when the early flights of green-wings and blue-wings come racing down the continent to linger a few weeks, then hurry on ahead of the cold.

I was involved with several friends in a duck lease 90 minutes south of the city—a shallow, muddy little pond of 40 or so acres, with two blinds. Some years there was too little water. Other years the creek flooded, overflowed the pond and washed the blinds away.

A few mornings each season, usually just before the freeze, the mallards—the big red-leg flight ducks—came in great numbers and the shooting was fine. Most days we watched them pass over high, looking for larger and more promising water. But it was the early teal opener that began the hunting year, and it was good to be down the road and out before first light, even if it seemed queer to be sitting in a duck blind in shirtsleeves.

Mainly I went out that morning for Rufus's benefit. That's how men often explain their hunting: They only do it out of obligation to the dogs. This time it was the truth.

To accustom him to sudden noise, I'd started by banging his food dish and rattling pans at feeding time. Then we graduated to a cap gun, and from that to blanks from a starter's pistol. The neighbors must have wondered why, with all that shooting, no ambulance ever came to the house.

He was ready now for the racket of some light shotgun loads at close range. So we loaded in the 3 o'clock morning dark, his crate and my chest waders in the back of the station wagon, him beside me on the front seat, and drove to the pond.

The sky was cloudless and full of stars. No one else was out that morning, so we would have the place to ourselves.

The blind was on the far bank, a waist-deep wade of most of a quarter-mile. Briefly I thought of trying to carry him out, Rufus under one arm, gun and bag of decoys in the other. But, loving water as he did, he plunged directly in and dog-paddled cheerfully beside me as we crossed.

The day came on with a rush—sparkling, windless, unpromising for ducks.

"Well, little fellow," I told Rufus, "maybe after while we'll let off a shot or two anyway, just to see how you like it."

I'd hardly said it when there was a whispering rush over the blind as a flight of a dozen green-wings sped in from behind, turned once and dropped on cupped wings straight to the decoys. My first startled shot went wild. The second put a drake in the water.

The surprise was what followed.

Except for songbirds in his yard and in the park, he'd never seen a feathered creature of any sort. But at the sound of the shot and the splash of the teal, Rufus was out of the blind and swimming for the prize.

He towed the duck in by its wing. And his expression, when I took it from him and lifted him back in with me, was both excited and proud. He sniffed the teal with interest, licked it once. Then, I swear, he looked skyward to see if there might be others coming.

"You're not a duck dog," I told him in a mock-chiding way. "You're a *bird dog!*"

He was not yet 6 months old. And I think it was in that moment that I understood, in a way I really hadn't before, that Providence had given me a very uncommon companion to share my seasons in the field.

NOVEMBER

O N TRIPS TO THE COUNTRY as the year turned he did more puppy things: chased grackle flocks, dug up field-mouse burrows, was not above pursuing a rabbit if one presented itself.

At home, he ate a library book and a potted flower. Then ate the flower's pot. He learned to sit atop his doghouse like the beagle in the cartoon, looking in through the kitchen window to be sure his bowl was being filled at the appointed hour.

And yet, from the beginning, he seemed to understand somehow the principal business of his life.

On our early walks, first in the park and then in a nearby patch of city woods, he'd never simply tagged along. He forged ahead, testing the limits as the best and the brightest are wont to do. Then I tied a quail wing to a fishing line and hid it in the grass for him to find.

Immediately, in those evening sessions on the lawn, he put his puppy ways aside. The scent of that wing—a last year's wing, saved over in the deep freeze—spoke a language in which he was born already eloquent. The look then in his golden eyes was remarkable to see.

On a sunny day, unseasonably hot for this month, I'd gone to the farm on an errand, and Rufus had ridden with me. Business finished, we set out to stretch our legs.

The quail, a solitary rooster, was in an unlikely place, on the face of a rocky slope below the field-stone foundation of a vanished homestead and the sprouty glades that must once have been that settler's little fields.

Possibly a rabbit, I thought as I walked in behind him, though I couldn't see one. *Or it could be a mouse.* Just under his nose, out of a tuft of weeds no larger than a saucer, the single bird burst up. Unready, I shot late and was lucky to fold him just before he topped the rise.

Rufus brought the bird to me as neatly as if we'd been doing this forever, and I let him mouth the quail a bit before I took it from him. I hugged him, relishing the moment, but he was restless to be off looking for the others. There weren't any others, though. Just the one—the first bird over the first point of his first season.

And there was better, much better, to come.

DECEMBER

THE WIND TURNED AROUND from the north, hard frost burned the vegetation brown, and those games played with the wing on a city lawn during spring and summer became real on a raw afternoon, in a brushy hedgerow along the crest between two emerald fields of winter wheat.

I was hunting with my longtime friend and newspaper colleague, Fred Kiewit, and two of Fred's regular quail-hunting pals. We'd prospected down an unproductive draw and were bound back up toward the road and the parked car, the wind at our backs, a covey of quail evidently running ahead in the high grass along the quarter-mile of hedge between the wheat fields.

Rufus was well out in front, working a section of the hedge back toward us, against the wind, then looping out and farther on to try a new section. He was smelling where the birds had been. Then where they had been more recently.

Then, finally, *where they were now.*

So intent we were in watching him that the covey, when it exploded just under his nose and ours, flew off all but unmolested.

The others spoke of it afterward—men in their 60s and 70s, old bird men and old dog men. Of how, in quail-hunters' language, he'd *set* the birds and held them. Of the style and steadiness of the point. Surely he wasn't a green pup, they said. Why, they'd seen dogs in their second and third season not work as well.

Rufus was indifferent to this praise. But I went a little giddy, like the father of some halfback who had just gone 70 yards through the Dallas Cowboys defense to win the Super Bowl.

That night I spent most of two hours trimming out cockleburs, hair by hair, from his tender underparts. It was a labor of pure devotion—in gratitude for which, the next day, he hid his dish again and ate another flowerpot. And then sat looking in from the roof of his house with pure devilment and pure puppy in his eyes.

We are not quite grown, yet, either of us. May these autumns of our extended childhoods be very long.

TWO
1 9 8 4

FEBRUARY

THERE IS MUCH THAT RUFUS does not yet understand. At 8 months, he knew perfectly the meaning of the birdy smell that came to his nose out of the long grass. He understood that interminable rides in cars with men were the prelude to that smell. And that the near, sharp reports of the men's guns were its invariable consequence.

In these affairs of business he was precocious. But about the commoner, out-of-season matters of simple living he remains an ungovernable truant.

He does not know why the humans of the house, while searching the yard for his dish, shout such strings of strident words when they stumble and go to their knees in the potholes he has made.

It puzzles him that the cats refuse to play, and instead peer out owl-eyed from under the furniture, uttering noises even nastier than the ones the humans make.

He refuses to accept that pillows and candles and wooden drawer-pulls are not for eating. He makes no distinction between the odd sock with a knot tied in it for his amusement, and the matched pair found tucked in shoes.

Cleanliness is nowhere on his agenda. He comes in from some enterprise in the cratered no man's land where, before his time, grass used to grow. His feet are mud to wrists and hocks. The floor and carpets record his passage. We noisily object, but he only seems glad for the attention.

Discipline is without noticeable effect. Stern words, in extreme cases a folded newspaper—they are as nothing to him. The only punishment of any use is banishment to the yard again. And then the craters grow deeper, the food dish goes farther into the bushes. In time, more mud comes in.

Last week he toyed with the notion of running away—leapt or scaled the fence into the neighbor's grounds behind, found himself in a fix and had to be rescued from that yard of larger dogs.

The boldness, so appealing in November, seems less a virtue in this closed and messy season. The yard is too small for Rufus. The house is too small for us all. Each afternoon I come home curious to find what else of mine will have entered his digestive tract.

I remind myself (when my wife, Katie, does not remind me) that he is mine by deliberate choice. That his craziness will finally pass. And that more and finer autumns of frozen mornings wait for us, if we both can last.

Meantime, I get no sympathy. Especially from friends who listen to the tales of ruin and opposing

wills, smile knowingly and nod like practiced sur-
vivors. It will get worse, they promise, before it gets
better. They have no experience with bird dogs,
some of those friends. But to them it all sounds terribly familiar.

They have raised, or are raising, adolescent sons.

MARCH

"THIS HOUSE IS GETTING CROWDED," I complained
the other day. "There's not even any place to
sit."

"What's wrong with your chair?" Katie asked.

"It's full."

"Full of what."

"Of dog."

"Oh," she said. "The *outdoor* dog?"

"That one."

"You could ask him to get down."

"He doesn't listen."

"Well, try asking *nicely*."

"I did. He growled at me."

That's what it has come to. The fenced yard stands
empty. His insulated house, custom-built at great
cost, is unslept in. My wife is on the dog's side, and
my little pretense of authority has become a joke.

It's only a matter of time until I will be served kibbles in a pan.

"He's a working dog," I have tried to argue. "He needs space and fresh air."

"Have you heard the temperature? The fresh air today is 5 degrees."

"All right, so it's a little brisk. He's made for it."

"Nonsense! Look at him. You can't tell me that's a 5-degree dog!"

He was listening to the talk about himself with one eye half-open.

"A lot of places in the world," I said, "dogs get cooked and eaten. Everywhere else they sleep outdoors. A dog in my chair is an unnatural thing."

"Cook and eat him if you want to. That's your business. But I'm not going to put him out in this weather."

So there's the choice I'm left with. Eat a bird dog, or spend most of the rest of my life sitting on the floor. And the problem about the chair is not the whole story. There's worse. When he appears to be sleeping, he really is waiting for a moment of inattention that will let him get the cats' food. And now he has taken to getting up at a hollow time of morning—between 3 o'clock and half-past—and demanding a run in the yard.

During daylight hours, the outdoors does not interest him. It's no good unless he can make me crawl trembling and cursing from bed to operate the door. I am lying snug under my blankets, eyelids fluttering in REM. And suddenly I realize that what I had thought was an erotic dream is only Rufus breathing hotly in my face to alert me to my duty. Those minutes spent standing barefoot on the cold kitchen linoleum are lonely and discouraging. The interruption of sleep is beginning to affect my work and even my health.

Usually my wife is undisturbed by these middle-of-the-night excursions. But last night, after more than an hour had passed, she noticed my side of the bed was empty and came downstairs to see what was keeping me.

"Is anything wrong?" she asked.

"Not really," I said—and kept turning the pages of the book.

"What in the world are you reading?"

"Nothing important."

"Isn't that a cookbook?"

"Well, actually ..." I was running my finger down the index. "Bearnaise sauce. Boeuf Bourguignon. Bouillabaisse. Bouillon. This is a punk recipe book!"

"What are you looking for?"

"There's nothing on Brittanys. It just skips from bread pudding straight to broccoli and brussels sprouts."

"You're disgusting," she said.

"Yes," I told her. "But I'm also very tired."

APRIL

OUR LIVES ARE suddenly rearranged.
Yesterday I went to lunch with the editor of the paper, Mike Waller, at whose suggestion six years ago this month I began writing my three-times-a-week column.

We enjoy one another's company, and generally there's no business of much substance to discuss, although he does sometimes ask, almost in a ritual way, what I see for the column in the year ahead. And I usually reply, "About what I saw for it last year."

Then we order our desserts, put the bill on the expense account and get back to work.

But when he asked that question yesterday, a bizarre and altogether unaccountable thing happened. I opened my mouth, and out came the words—unplanned, unconsidered—*"I think I'd like to live in Paris and write the column from there this year."*

There's no explaining it. It may have had something to do with the difficulty my daughters were having at school with their attempts to learn the

French language. Or, though they still were only 15 and 14, alarm at how quickly they were growing up, and a wish somehow to slow for a little while the clock of our lives together. Or possibly just a desire to experience fully one of the world's greatest cities—one I'd passed through a dozen times or more in my work, but had never had a chance to really know.

Or maybe it was a combination of all these things. But for whatever reason, the reckless, unexpected words were uttered.

"When would you plan to go?" Mike asked.

"June, I'm thinking. When the girls are out of school."

He turned it only briefly in his mind. "Well, put something on paper for me—what it's going to cost, what sort of stuff you'll be writing, that sort of thing. It sounds all right to me."

Then I had to go home and explain myself to Katie and our daughters, who did not know I was going to have this seizure at lunch.

There would be endless details to arrange: a school in Paris for the girls; someone to handle the day-to-day affairs of Katie's advertising business, while she consulted with clients by trans-Atlantic phone. But the pets were the biggest problem.

Friends invited one cat, the white one, to board

with them. A schoolteacher was found to live in the house and care for the three others and Cinnamon. But rambunctious Rufus was a problem of a different order. Fred Kiewit volunteered a solution. Fred had kept a succession of Brittanys, but when he lost his last and best one, Nixon, he hadn't the heart to begin with another. He'd hunted over Rufus, though, and was fond of him.

"I can't keep him at home," Fred said. "Vera wouldn't hear of it. But there's a kennel where I used to leave my dogs. It's clean, well run—a nice place out in the country. If you'll foot the kennel bill, I'll take him out for exercise as often as I can."

"And hunt him in the fall?"

"I don't know about that."

"This second year's important," I said. "I'd hate for him to miss the season."

"What if something happened—an accident?"

"It won't. I'd want you to hunt him like your own."

"I just don't know," Fred said.

"You have to promise that."

So it was settled. And in a crazy whirl of final preparations, we were away with 14 suitcases to the capital of the French.

AUGUST

WE'RE ESTABLISHED NOW in a pleasant apartment two blocks from the Seine, with a view down a tree-lined boulevard to a bridge and the forested hillside of the suburb of Saint-Cloud on the river's far side. And we have begun to feel at home in the neighborhood.

There are dogs of Rufus's breed—the *épagneul Breton*, as they say it—in great numbers here. This is, after all, the country where the breed originated.

Of course there are many other kinds, too, an almost infinite variety, many of them strange-looking beasts of indecipherable parentage. The Parisians, though most of them are apartment dwellers, are enormously fond of dogs. One of our amusements is to go down in the afternoon to a table at one of the cafes on the circle of our street, order a *café crème*, and watch the parade of folks passing along the sidewalk with their charges on leashes. My heart gives a little jump whenever a Brittany goes by.

One day, as we were driving south from Paris toward the Loire, across a great tableland of wheat fields where pheasants pecked for grit at the roadside, I saw a man walking at a field's edge, following a dog that at a distance, from his marking and carriage, could have been Rufus. The man had a shotgun in the crook of his arm, although in this month, with the season surely closed, I suppose he only carried it to feel somehow complete.

The butcher, Monsieur Leclerc, whose shop is just around the corner, also has a Brittany that passes its days napping either on the floor inside the shop's open front or on the sidewalk just out front. He describes the dog as *très calme*, and that is a great understatement. For, while the butcher's wife is a gaunt woman, the dog, like its master, is plump as a shoat, probably from the meat scraps, and of no imaginable use for hunting.

Monsieur Leclerc begins his mornings early with several glasses of Pernod at Le Clap's bar, a dingy place a couple of doors up our block. During the afternoon he switches to cognac. And in the evening, after closing, he crosses the street to the brasserie Le Narval, a more civil establishment, to top off his day with several beers. By then he is mellow, indeed.

I once made the mistake of mentioning to the butcher that I had a Brittany at home in the U.S.—an orange-and-white dog like his. Now, if I stop in late at Le Narval to buy tobacco or a box of matches and if Monsieur Leclerc happens to spy me, he rushes over, throws an arm around my shoulder and in a voice thick with emotion cries out to everyone in the place: "This American has a dog like mine!"

So that is my whole identity, how I am known in the neighborhood: the American with a dog like the butcher's. He does it every time—and every time I am reminded, with a little wrench, of Rufus.

DECEMBER

THE FAT ENVELOPE came under the apartment door with the rest of the morning's mail. The first snapshot was of Rufe on point in a field of milo, with new snow showing white between the rows. The next was of a man—Fred's good friend, Cliff—following Rufus through a patch of knee-high native grass. Then two men behind the dog on a snowy country lane. Then a couple of Rufus in full stride, looking wonderfully fit. Then a picture of two men, guns at the ready, walking in behind him on another point. Finally, a shot of one of the men and Rufe at a distance, walking together, the man with a pheasant in hand.

The letter in which they were folded had a journalist's economy.

Here are a few pictures. But—as you can see—there are no prize-winners among them. Best regards, Fred K.

It was no wonder the pup looked in such splendid shape. For when I spoke to the office by phone, a friend told me that every day since we'd left in June, Fred had made the drive to the kennel—a round-trip of nearly 70 miles—to give Rufus an hour's early run in the cool of the morning.

"I did it for myself," Fred would tell me another time. "For the pleasure of it."

"But *every day?*"

"Well, you said to treat him like my own."

I didn't miss the office a bit that year. We didn't even miss our house, because our apartment looking out on the river was home now. But we missed our animals terribly. Katie sometimes dreamed of the cats, and I dreamed of being out somewhere in a Midwestern autumn field with Rufus.

Every time we woke with a momentary regret, but then it passed. In Paris no regret lasts very long.

THREE
1 9 8 5

JUNE

HOW MUCH DO animals know? How much do they remember?

With golden eyes as cool as ice he stared out through the wire of his kennel at the stranger coming toward him.

For his first 15 months of life he'd had a regular home—a yard, his own food dish, a park for exercise, a rug indoors for inclement nights. Then he'd had to be boarded out, kenneled in a place with dozens of other dogs, a clamorous company, and given over to the companionship of another man.

What sense did he make of that? None, most likely. One morning he was loaded in the car, as so many happy times before. And after traveling awhile he was taken out and led past other boarders raging at their wires, and locked in an empty pen. And the car and the man went unexplainably away.

After that the other man, the different one, came regularly. In the autumn they would spend a day or two days together looking for quail and pheasants. Then he would go back to the pen. Autumn turned to bitter winter. There was straw in his box, and maybe he slept warm, or maybe not. Certainly there was no rug on a heated floor. A year he spent there, and that was nearly half his life so far—long enough you would think he might have forgotten all that went before.

Now this stranger was walking toward his pen and, for a fact, in those flat, golden eyes there was not a sign of recognition.

I put down a hand. A nose was thrust cautiously toward it. There was a moment's uncertainty. Then his face turned up—looked directly into mine. The yellow eyes were no longer cool, detached. There was familiarity in them. They were full of things recalled.

His time away is finished now. But what can he possibly understand of this strange experience? Nothing, I suppose, although surely he will remember it. Any creature that remembers home must also remember exile. Nor is he apt ever to forget that other man whose visits and excursions gave purpose to those weeks.

What he does seem to understand is that the exile is over—not just interrupted but really finished. Perfectly unperturbed, he sleeps again on his rug or in his chair, as if he'd never left them. When called to ride in the car he goes gladly, expecting only good, never imagining he might again be left.

My explanation of all of this would be lost on him, and anyway he does not seem to require one. Intuition tells him all he needs to know. He's home.

He sleeps warm. And that's how it will always be. Some men learn about forgiveness by studying the lives of saints. And some of us keep dogs.

JULY

DURING THOSE MONTHS when our household was in a state of disassembly, I spent much time picturing the tenderness of all our reunions.

But the white cat, who used to rule the place, has come home with a bit of a limp. And the black-and-white one, alert to the disability and seeing his chance for power, scowls and struts shamefully, hogging the food. So the white one has turned for solace to the gray one. But the gray one, whose memory is short, takes those overtures for a threat—hissing at him open-mouthed, sending him off discouraged into the jungle of the hall coat closet.

Cinnamon is glad to see the white cat, but is less pleased to have unruly Rufus back. For a heady time, there, she thought she was shut of him. Now she goes about sad-eyed on three legs, while Rufus growls with pleasure and carries her fourth leg—the off-hind one—in his jaws. The white cat would like to associate with Cinnamon, but that would mean coming out of the coat closet and getting past Rufus and the black-and-white cat to do it. And the rewards of a washed ear don't justify the risks of that.

The rituals of feeding have become enormously more complicated. Instead of coming all together to one counter, the cats must be fed now in separate rooms. And the dogs, too—not because the pup will steal the old one's food, which he's certainly not above doing, but because the very sight of Rufus takes her appetite.

Sleeping arrangements are similarly segregated. The black-and-white cat sleeps in the basement, with the door latched to keep him from attempting a middle-of-the-night coup d'etat against the crippled king. The gray cat wants to sleep on the bed, as was her habit, unless the white cat is on it already. In which event she marches downstairs to sulk on the sofa.

Cinnamon would not mind sharing the bed with the white cat if she could extract her leg from Rufe's jaws long enough to heave herself up onto it. There is a cage with a lock for Rufus, but if he is put inside he whines piteously and without end, depriving me of sleep and setting the nerves of all the others so on edge that when they reassemble in the morning, fights immediately break out. Rufus therefore sleeps wherever he wants and empties the food dishes impartially, giving rise to mews of righteous hunger and further grudges.

I had never thought of our house as especially cramped, but as I move the pieces around on this complicated board I am running out of strategies. Worse, I am running out of rooms. Maybe things will get better. Maybe, with a little patience, the former patterns of coexistence will be rediscovered or relearned.

But it will have to happen fairly soon, because one day Katie and the girls, who stayed on in France after me, will be coming home. That is, they're *supposed* to. I had looked forward to that as the final, happy stage of the reunion. And don't misunderstand. I still do want them back, provided the situation straightens itself out.

There's nothing I'd hate worse to have to do than sit down and write a letter saying, fond as I am of them, there's just no place left to fit them in.

OCTOBER

FOR HIM, A DOG OF PURPOSE, the lush verdancy of summer was mostly nuisance and confusion.

The air was rank with the cloying stink of growing stuff—of clipped grass and petunias in their pots and honeysuckle clambering at the fence. If those smells can fill a man's nose, what must they be to his? As overpowering, surely, as the background clamor of passing trucks to a sightless man who listens at an intersection for the click of the changing light.

But now, in frosty nights and crisp days, in the withering down and drying of the season, the message carried to him on the air has begun to resolve itself into a sense of something he remembers and understands.

In his yard, morning through afternoon, he supervises the activities of squirrels. Squirrels, he knows, are not his proper business. In the long generations of arriving at who he is, squirrels somehow were factored out. But there is an even older memory, of a time when *being dog* was an undiscriminating vocation.

He marks the nimble creatures' passage from utility wire to walnut branch to garage roof, and thence to some invisible universe beyond. His stare is fixed and cool.

From earliest puppyhood he's had those strange eyes. Soft-natured and playful he is, a tail-wagging terror-slave of the smallest kitten. Yet sometimes when he turns his gaze on you there is the fleeting, odd sensation that his eyes are not windows, as Cinnamon's are. The color, exactly, of Baltic amber, they see all but give nothing back. It is like looking at a one-way glass.

What's really in his thoughts, then, I can only guess, or speculate about from other small signs.

Such as the way he wastes no time now with vain territorial markings, but instead plunges straight into the rattling undergrowth of the yard's perimeter—seeking, seeking.

Or, when believing himself alone and unobserved, the way he will stand for minutes on end, his head raised, drinking from the city wind a cocktail of autumn samples, perhaps in the hope, against all odds, of detecting among them the one fragile scent that drives him and gives him meaning.

Now, I know the feelings, ranging from indifference to outright hostility, that the act of hunting evokes in some folk. And that's fine. They can think about it whatever they like. But for more than half my life I have kept hunting dogs of different breeds, hunters of different game. And have cared about them not just for themselves but also in a more abstract way—something close to admiration—because of the intensity, the single-mindedness by which at some level their lives are absolutely ruled.

Loving they may be. They might even beg a biscuit or roll over to be scratched. But some part of them is never quite a pet. Some part is private and fiercely self-possessed. So I do not resent the slight distance established between us by those cool, yellow eyes. Why should anyone be threatened by dignity in a dog?

NOVEMBER

THE ESSAYS WRITTEN IN PARIS have become a book. And books—not just the writing of them but later the going out to read from them and talk about them—can take a lot of time. So the other day while I was busy with that, Rufus opened the quail season with Fred Kiewit and some other men.

It was a fine fall morning, cold and gray and dampish—the sort of morning when the birds hunker close in the weeds and the smell carries strong. On a day like that, the dog is a flash of color devouring the fields without effort, and even an old hunter's legs work properly until far on in the afternoon.

That's how I remember it. But of course I have no recent experience in these things.

There is a myth promoted among the young, which suggests that if they work faithfully at whatever tasks bad luck and their meager talents dictate, then one day they will claw their way onto a plateau of ease. And will be able, finally, to do the things they really wanted to do for the first 50 or so years of their lives.

The promise is wonderfully enticing. But experience shows it generally to be false. I have a friend who, in the prime of his ability, manages the affairs of an important company. He is, by all the world's conventional measures, a huge success. We enjoy being together, even if the relentless press of his responsibilities makes the chance for that infrequent. He speaks sometimes of the adventures he would like to take, which his means would easily permit but for which he has no time.

He is not struggling to make something of himself. He has *arrived*. And arrival has exacted its price.

Another friend travels the country and the world, advising giant corporations about how they might reorganize their affairs to achieve not only more productivity but also greater satisfaction in the lives of all those associated with the enterprise. He, too, is wonderfully successful at what he does.

During the times when he is at home—sometimes for a whole weekend, sometimes only for a few snatched hours between planes— we speak again of something we'd planned to do, usually in the season that, amazingly, has already slipped past. We make another plan. We vow this time we'll hold to it—we really will. But even as we say that, he is repacking to rush to the airport. And I am thinking ahead to the tyranny of another year's writing deadlines to be met, with all the words still unfound.

When Rufus came home from his two-day opening of the season with other hunters, he was scratched and sore-footed and ready for some heavy-duty sleeping. But he had about him a manner of sweet completion.

I wanted to tell him how I once thought the finest thing might be to be a fishing guide somewhere in the north country, or just a squatter in a forest cabin, with no bell to answer, no clock except the day-breaks and sunsets of the seasons as they turned. I wanted to ask him, because I could not quite remember, how the damp fields smelled and how the birds sounded as they burst from cover.

But he wouldn't have answered. Too happy for talking, he just nodded off.

FOUR
1 9 8 6

JANUARY

THERE'S A SMALL FARM only an hour north of the city whose every field and ravine I know. It holds two dependable coveys, and sometimes a third. As last year rushed toward its end, that's where Rufus and I managed to escape—sometimes only the two of us, sometimes with a friend—for several half-day hunts between the busyness with the new book. There's a moment from the last of those outings that I remember especially.

In an upland wild-grass meadow we'd found one of the coveys and gotten a bit of shooting. Then we worked down to lower ground along the creek. Cattle had grazed there, and the cover was scant—an unpromising place for birds. Rufus cast over the area quickly, nose high to the wind. Then, whirling in midstride, he plunged over the sheer creek bank into the water below, bearded with a rim of ice, and came down on point on the one dry little hummock in the middle.

I looked at the place from above. That islet around which the creek divided and then rejoined was three square yards in area at most. Past floods had scoured it. The only vegetation was a single bush you could have covered with a bushel basket, and logic said no quail could be there. But it pays to believe the dog.

The bank was too steep and slippery to get down, so I walked along it most of a quarter-mile until I found a reasonable descent. Then I made my way along the creek bed, jumping from one dry place to the next, trying to keep from soaking my boots. Fifteen minutes it must have taken me, maybe longer. Rufus had not moved an inch, though as I walked up behind I could see him quivering a bit from having held the point so long.

Well, naturally there *was* a quail in that solitary little bush. And of course, in surprise at what could not be so, I missed the bird as it flew straight away. Rufus looked at me with an expression of reproach and disbelief. And so we closed the book on a year of too few hunts.

Luckily, the Missouri season runs on to middle January. Sometimes this late hunting is splendid. Other years the weather turns wretched, and men and dogs retire to the comfort of the stove.

I'd promised a friend's son an end-of-season outing. He was eager to get out for a day and watch the dog work, maybe get a shot or two. The night before last, an arctic front blew in and the thermometer sank away to minus 7. But the day's forecast was for clearing and sun. If at all possible, the promise needed to be kept.

Yesterday morning was brutal, the sun watery and

weak. Dressed for it, we were not too uncomfortable. Rufus found a large covey scattered in a plum thicket. They held tight in that weather, and came up singly, so that every few paces there was another point. I took a couple of birds, and my young companion was pleased to drop one.

We passed out of the brush, then into a small patch of cut milo. And in a shallow ditch that cut across the field we made a sad discovery. In hard winter, quail bunch close together on their ground roost, their pooled body heat a defense against the cold. But the night's terrible temperature, coupled with a cutting wind, had been too much for the birds we found in the bottom of the wash. There were ten of them, frozen hard as stones in their tight little circle.

I hadn't the heart for more shooting.

"This weather could last several more days," I told the boy. "We'd better quit hunting, and give the ones that can a chance to make it through."

I whistled Rufus in, and we went together into the oak woods for a half-day's walk through a timbered valley where it was unlikely we'd disturb any huddled birds. The trees were black as ink strokes against the folds of the land, dusted white with the night's powdery snow. The boy was refreshed, his spirit lighter as we hiked back to the car. And that was the point of our going.

That night, cleaning the gun while Rufus slept on the floor beside me, next November seemed an eternity away.

MARCH

"THIS IS DENNIS MAGGART," said the voice on the phone. "I don't know if you remember me."

"Of course. And I remember your Maggie. How's she hunting?" I asked.

"Great. Just great. I had her in Iowa and South Dakota. Lots of birds early. She's going to be a good one. How about Rufus?"

"Better than I deserve," I told him.

"What I'm calling about," Dennis said, "is we've decided to let Maggie have a litter. Have you ever thought about breeding Rufus?"

I hadn't—though the idea may have crossed Rufus's mind.

"When we were talking about it," he said, "we couldn't help remembering the two of them as pups."

"When does Maggie come in season?"

"It should be next month."

"Well, I think I can promise you Rufus is willing."

"What kind of stud fee would you want?"

"We're amateurs," I told him. "I wouldn't know what to ask."

"How about the pick of the litter?"

"Sure. I might have a friend in mind for that pup," I said. "Give me a call when it's time."

APRIL

THERE IS, AMONG the creatures we patronizingly call dumb, a surprising amount of understanding. Call it only intuition, if you like. But by whatever name, the display of it sometimes is amazing.

The white cat met misfortune the other day and came home groggy and disabled. It was, luckily, a problem whose effects would pass. But for that day and several afterward he was a deplorable case, unable to stand and walk or even, at first, to raise his head. We installed him in the bedroom on a pallet of towels with a cover over him for warmth. From his nest he peered out helplessly, eyes lusterless and confused.

Evening came, the hour when Rufus is brought in from his yard to enjoy the touch of hands and take his greater ease in upholstered chairs. The white cat, in the fullness of his powers, is nothing to be trifled with. He's a heavyweight in the Marciano mold. The sound that issues from his chest when he's annoyed can turn a challenger's blood to ice. But that's when he's himself.

The pitiful thing in the towel bundle was perfectly defenseless. So how would the others respond? Would they take it as a time for settling accounts? And how about Rufus especially? He bore no grudges that we knew of. But his one gait is an incorrigible romp, badly suited to a sickroom. We took the chance, though, and let him in.

One bound inside the bedroom door and he stopped—just stopped stock-still, nose thrust slightly forward to identify the patient, his face (for animals' features can be wonderfully expressive) mystified and grave. Sitting, then, Rufus raised one forepaw as if to playfully box. There was no motion from the bundle. The glazed eyes remained slitted nearly shut. The paw was lowered, and the dog sat a moment longer, considering.

You no doubt have read how elephants will stay with a stricken member of the band, and even after death will use their trunks to try to urge the fallen individual to regain its feet and continue on the march. Well, that's just what Rufus did next. He drew close on soft pads, reached out his nose and with a gentleness quite uncommon for him, administered several little nudges that said, plain as anything: *Get*

*up. It's wrong to see you lying there so still. I'll bet you can get
up if you'll only try.*

But the white cat was beyond any such effort. He
just drifted in his daze, and gave no sign.

Whereupon the dog lay down exactly beside him,
parallel and very near, but with face turned a bit sideways so that he could notice any stirring. At that
moment, for whatever reason, he preferred that
place on the floor to his usual one.

Katie came up from downstairs, then, and reported the strange behavior of the other cats. Mostly
they're individuals and not much on collaboration.
They keep a civil distance, although that's not how
she had just found them.

"They're all sitting on the hall carpet," she said.
"Close together in a kind of circle, as if they'd been
talking it over."

It can get crowded, sharing a house with so many
others of such different wants and shapes. Crowded
and sometimes inconvenient. But two legs or four,
clever or dumb, we're there for one another when
caring's of any use.

MAY

I'VE HAD ANOTHER of those lunches with the editor of the newspaper, and this time when he asked what plans I had for the column, I'd considered my reply in advance.

"Africa," I said. "I think I'd like to write from there for several months. Not about politics. About the lives of the small Africans, the ordinary people."

We all pass through life with more than one agenda. It has seemed to me that a useful function of journalism, or any sort of writing, is to enable a reader in some way to experience a variety of other places in the world, and the people who live there, and the joys and troubles that shape their days—things that the reader might not otherwise have the chance to know.

That's my public agenda, the one I speak about to editors.

The private one is that I am raising two daughters. And like any parent I hope before they are grown and gone to arm them with some of the experiences I've found helpful in trying to understand the world. In the early 1960s, when I was a very young newspaperman, an editor sent me to Africa to travel for several months and write about the storm of new independence—the "wind of change," as it was called—that had swept across much of the continent.

I began to learn, on that journey, the variety of people with whom we are privileged and doomed to share the planet. Africa affected me powerfully. I had been back there at least a half-dozen times since, although never to do precisely the kind of writing I now had in mind. And I wanted to give my daughters the gift that editor had given me so many years ago.

After more discussion the plan was approved.

"We're going away again," I told Fred Kiewit on the phone.

"How long?"

"Only through September. But I'll have to kennel Rufus. Could you look in on him again from time to time."

"Sure," said Fred. "Don't worry about him."

"There's another thing. You said one time you wish you had a Rufus pup. Well, there are going to be some—they'll come while we're away. The pick of the litter is yours."

"Lord knows I'd love to have one," he said. "But Vera would never hear of it."

"Sure she would."

"Believe me," he said. "There's no way. I couldn't keep him at the house. And I wouldn't have a dog whose whole life was spent in a kennel."

"Maybe Vera will change her mind. And even if

she doesn't you could take him out every day, the way you did with Rufus while we were in France."

"I don't know."

There was a long silence as he turned the possibilities in his mind.

"Let me think about it," he said. "She'd never forgive either one of us."

But I knew from the way he said it the pup would have a home.

SEPTEMBER

MAIL SERVICE IS SLOW and somewhat chancy to and from most places in Africa, unless you have the luck to find a *pigeon*, as journalists call a traveler into whose hands they can press a dispatch. Thus it was middle September before the letter came.

And it was characteristically brief.

A fine litter, Fred wrote. *Six pups. Named him Rusty. He's going to be on a Hallmark card. Out with Rufe every day. See you in a month or so. Fred*

The U.S. postmark was mid-August. Actually, I was leaving in a little more than a week.

OCTOBER

LIKE MOST OTHERS of his kind, Rufus gets worthless and a little crazy in the idle months, but he has begun again to sober and steady. It always happens when the days shorten and the nights cool.

He sits for long minutes, his eyes trained unblinking on the birds that trespass through the airspace of the yard. He knows their name: *Bird*. After his own name, it was the first word in his slim vocabulary. He also knows they are not exactly the right bird, but they are alike enough to be suggestive. He watches them, waits until they pass from view, then watches for the next ones. I don't know how much, if anything, he understands of time. But the changing light and the different smell of the paling grass are signs he can read perfectly.

This autumn is his fourth—the fourth of the eight or 10 good ones he will have. After that, with luck, it will be just the house, the rug, the soft bedroom chair. He loves that chair now with an intensity that is almost lascivious. But when those later autumns come and his legs won't carry him fast or far, he'll love it less.

It's another busy year. The calendar gets cluttered. There isn't really time enough for truant days spent wandering across fields, fording creeks, shouldering through underbrush. Too much of that can chill a marriage, cripple a career. One has to have priorities.

But on the other hand ...

It's not just a wife and a boss a man has to live with. He also has to live with himself. A long time ago I had two beagle friends. We must have spent a couple of hundred days afield together, and they fed me well on fat rabbits. Then life changed. I got distracted by other things for what seemed a minute, and when I looked again they were white-muzzled and sore of leg.

After they were gone, it wasn't the rabbits they'd run that I remembered. It was all the ones they *hadn't* run because I'd imagined I had other more important responsibilities. That's more guilt than anyone ought to have to carry.

Rufus has a gift, a calling. It would be pure selfishness, I tell myself, to put my work ahead of his. He goes now, at evening, to his place on the upholstery. He whines a little in his sleep, and his feet twitch as he runs through some birdy dream. He may suspect a certain splendid morning is near. Is it possible he knows that morning is tomorrow?

The years will go like leaf smoke, and with them any record of our misbehavior. We'll have a long time, he and I, to remember the best of autumn and learn to hate the chair.

NOVEMBER

W E OPENED THE SEASON at the little north farm and have gotten back there several times during the month. On every hunt we've found quail. The two coveys are dependable as the sunrise. One is in the timbered draw between two fields below the house. The other is in a weedy patch of waste ground below a pond. If we find a third, it will be in the switchgrass field.

Bernard Mead, the man who farms there, is a friend. Two miles to the west is his son's farm, a larger tract. By limiting the number of birds we take, these handy places should see us through the best part of the season.

I had a phone call the other day from a man named Stuart Mitchelson. He's a lawyer—an older man, in his 70s, I believe. He proposed a hunt with Rufus and his setter, Dolly. You never know how it will go, hunting with a stranger, but he sounded congenial, and we set a day.

The weather turned warm, the dogs labored, and we found few birds. But Mitch turned out to be the sort of man one is lucky to spend time with—devoted to quail hunting, with a lifetime's good stories to tell, and sturdy in the field in spite of having had a heart attack several years ago. By afternoon, the morning's stranger was a valued friend. We planned another outing before Christmas.

DECEMBER

LUCK WAS AGAINST US. The freezing mist that glazed the windshield during a two-hour drive we could have endured. But just as we pulled to a stop on a gravel lane, with a likely mix of weedy wasteland and crop fields stretching away on either side, the skies opened and the mist became a frigid deluge.

We tried—let Rufus and Dolly out, and pulled our collars up. But we hadn't gotten out of sight of the car before our gloves were wet and icy rivulets were running down our backs inside our shirts.

"I don't think I can take much of this," Mitch said. "I'm sorry."

"Don't be," I told him. Though he had 20 years on me, my gratitude was very great. "This isn't supposed to be about suffering."

We called in the dogs and hurried back to the comfort of the car heater.

"There's a place I'd like to show you next year," said Mitch. "Good people, and a world of quail."

"I'll count on it," I told him.

That's how you can bear the sorrow of a season's ending, by looking always forward to the next.

FIVE
1987

APRIL

WHEN WE BOUGHT the house 15 years ago, the yard was enclosed by a 4-foot metal fence. Never once, since joining us, had Cinnamon ever challenged it. With Rufus 4 now, well past his puppyhood, I'd begun to think of him as dependable.

I was wrong. After he'd jumped it once and gotten a taste for roaming, the fence presented exactly the same impediment to him that it would to a hawk.

Usually he waited until I had left for the office or gone out of town. Then he sailed over for a look at the wider world. A couple out jogging spied him hunting along a wooded creek bank in a neighborhood of grand houses most of a mile away. Another time a woman called to report that he'd come to visit her five dogs, and that all seemed to enjoy the new acquaintance.

Once, while I was away from the city, he disappeared for two whole days. Katie, frantic, tacked up pleading signs on every utility post for blocks around; called all the agencies, municipal and private, concerned with straying critters; asked the postman, Ernie, to keep an eye out while he made his rounds. None of it was any use. She dreaded having to give me the news when I came home.

But on the morning of the third day, when she

went downstairs to make her first cup of coffee, there was his face at the door glass. Evidently tired of the vagabond life, he'd found his way home, leaped over the fence and into the yard, and, showing no remorse, was impatient for breakfast to be served.

"We've been awfully lucky," Katie said. "But this can't go on."

"We'll figure something out," I told her. "I'll make a call or two and get some estimates on a higher fence."

JUNE

"GUESS WHO JUST TOOK another tour of the neighborhood," my wife announced when I came home from work.

"Who?" I said—and felt a kind of giddiness come over me. Because I knew the answer already.

From his place at the patio door, where he likes to watch the fat squirrels as they rob the feeder, Rufus turned to follow this conversation about himself. His expression was heavy with sorrow at his own wretchedness.

"I let him out for a little run in the yard," Katie said. "When I found him, he was in front of a house on the next street over."

"How?" I asked.

"How what?"

"How did he get out?"

"Why, he went over, naturally."

I clutched the breakfast room table for support and looked through the window at the new wooden yard fence, taller than a man's head, built only a few weeks ago at significant cost for the sole purpose of keeping Rufus from taking tours of the neighborhood.

"No," I said. "He's found a loose board somewhere. Or else he dug under. He didn't go over."

"Look for yourself."

So I did. I went out and wandered the whole perimeter, stumbling through mud and worse, disoriented in the way you'd be if you came home one evening from the office and found a convenience store where your house ought to be.

A fence like mine is the final solution, the A-bomb in the war against rambling. No dog looked upon by the eye of man ever jumped one. But there weren't any loose boards. And no signs of tunneling. I went back indoors.

"Well?" she said.

"He climbed it."

"Don't be silly. Dogs don't climb smooth boards, seven feet straight up."

"He used a ladder, then."

"Where would he get a ladder? We don't even own one."

"Or else he has discovered the power of wingless flight."

"Sit down," Katie suggested. "Take a deep breath. Have a glass of water or something. I don't like to see you so worked up."

"Who's worked up?"

"Maybe you could take a little nap before dinner."

"No," I told her, as I let the mystery beast out into the yard. "I'm going to sit right here by the window until I see how he does it."

"How long?"

"As long as it takes."

He walked around in the yard, trying to give an impression of total innocence. Occasionally he glanced at the top of the fence. Mostly he watched me watching him from the window.

"It's starting to get dark," Katie said after a while.

"That's all right. There's always tomorrow. Sooner or later he'll make a mistake."

"He's very smart, you know."

"Meaning by that?"

"Meaning nothing," she said. "You're smart, too. But you have a lot on your mind. He can *concentrate*."

"Are you saying he's won?"

"Not really," she said. "It's a nice fence—a pretty fence. Now let's just call him an indoor dog and get on with our lives."

Later analysis yielded one possible explanation. It was perhaps conceivable—though hardly credible—that he had gotten on the roof of his house and had used that as the launching pad for his flight to freedom. But that would have required a standing leap of four feet laterally and another four vertically in order to catch the fence top with his forepaws and drag himself over.

It was an utterly unimaginable gymnastic. But to be sure, I built a chicken-wire barrier atop his house to prevent him from getting up there. And, for a fact, his career as a tourist ended.

AUGUST

THE BIRD DOG is lost again.

Not lost in the literal, physical sense. He's still around, and still a friend. But I have lost him as a useful working animal, which hunting dogs are supposed to be. It happened during this summer's spell of blistering heat when he discovered air conditioning.

The bedroom has a window unit. When the awful

heat came, he immediately noticed the difference between the pleasant nights in his chair and the sweltering days outside. And it occurred to him he might correct this situation. Were not the cats in there and cool? Was not the old dog snoozing in the lap of air-conditioned comfort? Then why should he, a dog of real utility, provider of fowl for the family table, not have some of this luxury?

He pressed his hopeful face against the outer glass, but our hearts were hard. To present his case in a more dramatic way, he began sitting on a patio table, glaring in accusingly at eye level through a kitchen window. It yielded nothing, though. He remained outside.

So he learned to open the back door. That's right, *learned to open it himself!* One afternoon I looked up from my typewriter and there he was, indisputably inside, looking immensely pleased by his new competence. As far as he's concerned, the case is closed. He's in where it's cool, and it's not negotiable. He makes himself as small as possible and rarely moves.

The other day Katie called him, suggesting it might be time to trot outside on a sanitary errand. He didn't budge—just looked around the room to see if, by some coincidence, she might be speaking to another dog of the same name. So I called him, and he growled.

As you probably know, the main virtue of a fine bird dog, apart from a keen nose, is unquestioning obedience. The master's command is his highest law. Defiance is unthinkable. He is indifferent to the elements. If game is downed, he will endure any discomfort to find and bring it to hand. In a word, there is nothing a bird dog will not do for his master.

Wrong! This one will not even leave his chair in an air-conditioned room.

When he was chosen from his littermates several years ago, I was looking for a pup with intelligence and staying power. That's exactly what I got. Rufus is no fool. And he's staying cool.

NOVEMBER

THE SKY IS DEEPEST BLUE, the light strong. Dry leaves rattle in the gusts of morning wind. The air, clarified now of the summer's green confusions, is rich with the musk of furred and feathered things. The season is nearly a week gone. And though Rufus cannot count the days, he knows the autumn is not proceeding as it ought to.

Impatient, he waits, watching the impudent squirrel that chatters from its branch, listening for the lifting of the door to the garage, from which his travel crate is carried forth to the car at moments of importance.

Coming in at evening, he canvasses the house for any hopeful signs: boots set out in readiness, a hunting coat hanging on a doorknob, the sharp smell of gun oil through the fabric of the case. But none of that he finds. It is just a night like any other, presaging another wasted day like all the rest. Discouraged, he arranges himself on the rug, one eye open and following every movement, missing nothing, on the slight chance he might be wrong.

I've gotten restless, too—impatient less for myself than for the dog, who deserves better than to be kept and caged by someone who's caged in other ways, by time and imagined duties. But why make so much of this? What's a week, anyway?

The trouble is that lives are processes that can be measured. And when lives are short, the measurement gets fierce. He's now in his fifth autumn. By age 8 or 9 he'll be past the best of it—the capacity for sudden easy flight across the fields gone out of him. The days of the chase will be fewer, and will end in weariness.

This season and another four good ones he'll likely have. Each season with 10 or 11 weeks. The calculation is easy, too easy. Of the balance of his life— that is, of the time of year he *lives for*—almost a one-fiftieth part already has been lost during a week in which I imagined I had other things to do.

But that's about to be corrected.

I'm working strange hours now—writing short and fast. Letters of complaint, if there are any, will pile up unread on the desk. And if my employers want to scold me for that or any other reason, they'll have to find me first.

DECEMBER

THIS SEASON HAS LAID IN for man and dog a fine store of memories to carry us through. All the moments were rich. One was utterly magical.

There was a grand hunt with my new friend, Mitch, at his favorite place, the farm of George and Mary Frank outside the town of Westphalia, Kansas. George used to be a devoted bird hunter himself until he lost a leg in a combine accident. But he still is excited by the whistle of quail, and deliberately leaves grain standing at the field edges after harvest as food for them in the hard weather. He's pleased to have friends enjoy the land.

The Franks are a large family. One son has stayed in the area to take over much of the active farming. The eight other grown children have gone out into the world to careers as a school psychologist, a teacher, a psychiatrist, a school administrator, a nurse, a surgeon, an engineer and an ophthalmologist. George and Mary are the sort of people who insist that hunters must come to the house for a midday break and a country meal so stupendous that the walking in afternoon is noticeably slower.

That chilly morning, Rufus pointed three large coveys in the *first half-mile* of fence row. By day's end he'd found 18 coveys. So plentiful were the quail that it soon was clear we'd have to limit our shooting if we meant to stretch the hunt. After that we alternated, each one taking a covey rise alone, and rarely hunting down the singles. We covered several miles, all on the Franks' land, and circled back at the end beside a little field near the car.

We both were leg-sore and eager to sit, but Rufus wasn't finished. He vaulted the fence and almost immediately locked on point.

"I guess I'd better go in there," I said wearily. "But I'm only doing it for the dog."

"I know," Mitch said, wryly—and he would chuckle about it again on every later hunt. *"It's only for the dog."*

There were some good outings, though shorter, to Bernard's place north of town. But the moment of absolute magic occurred on my farm two hours to the south. I've since told several longtime bird hunters about it, and not one of them remembers ever seeing what I saw that day.

I'd driven to the farm in the morning, and had been occupied much of the day with chores and business. The afternoon was getting well along when Rufus and I, just the two of us, set out together for a favored place—an old fence row, choked with berry brambles and thickets of wild plum, separating two fields of native grass.

Nearly always we could find a covey there, but this time the birds were absent. It didn't matter. The hour was fine, with the shadows long and the winter sky paling to lemon through the bare scaffolding of the oak woods at the field's far side.

We took the short way back toward the cabin, angling across the field, waist high in tawny grass. Then I saw Rufus wheel and brake, face thrust forward, quivering with intensity. I stepped in beside and ahead of him, ready for the sudden rush of wings.

But it wasn't a covey that came up around us. It was a multitude! By the 20s and 50s they rose, and the sound of their rising startled others—waves of them exploding out of the tall grass and tilting away *en masse* on set wings to the field's edge and on into the timber. I can't begin to say how many quail there were in that amazing congregation, but certainly more than 150, maybe 200, maybe more. Nor can I begin to guess what coincidence or combination of conditions had brought those 20 or so coveys together to seek their night's roost in that single small field.

The memory of that will fill my imagination always, as I'm sure the gathered scent of so many quail must have filled Rufus's nose.

I never raised the shotgun and he never moved an inch from where he'd come to point. We just stood together there, transfixed with amazement by something neither of us will ever see again.

SIX
1988

MARCH

BRILLIANCE IS A powerful asset. Wealth, if you're lucky enough to have it, can open some doors. But when it comes to getting ahead in the important things, patience is the sovereign virtue.

Take Rufus, for instance. He's about as bright as he needs to be, though you wouldn't call him a genius. And he's certainly not rich. But he has a clear idea of how he wants to live and is willing to advance toward his goal by measured stages.

In the beginning, as I've said, there was the dog-house. His destiny, it had been decided, was as an outdoor dog. He disagreed. Standing first on the roof of his house, and later on the patio table, he could look directly through a window and see the old dog, happy on her rug, and indoor people and a quantity of indoor cats. The logic of his being an outdoor dog escaped him. But there was a closed door between him and all that comfort, and he was small.

With bird dogs as with buffalo calves, however, the smallness is self-correcting. It just takes time. So he waited, and when his stature permitted he destroyed the door and came inside. Once in, he discovered that the old dog, the people and the cats spent their evenings in an upstairs bedroom. He was allowed to join them, provided he remained politely on the floor.

It did not escape his notice that the cats arranged themselves on the bed and, when the hour grew late, the people joined the cats and the old dog selected one of the people's soft chairs—chairs that for unfathomable reasons were forbidden him. He brooded for a time on this injustice. Then he realized that the people slept, and that what happened while they slept was unimportant to them.

If he was seen to be on the floor when the light went out, and again when the alarm sounded and the people stirred, he would be praised as a floor dog, not a chair dog. The quality of his nights improved. But the arrangement was limiting. Sometimes he liked to sleep in the daytime, too. Or in the evening hours before the people retired. So he began insinuating himself into the chair whenever it pleased him.

The people grew used to it. They learned to watch television sitting on footstools, while Cinnamon and the bird dog slept in the chairs.

There remained the issue of the bed. He leapt up there the first time barking an alarm, pretending to scare a burglar from the yard. Sometimes after that he sat on the bed to look through the window at rabbits among the flowers. When the people remembered they commanded him to get down. In time they remembered less often. Climbing the stair they would hear the thump of him leaving that unauthorized place. But when they came in the room he would be in his chair, the soul of innocence.

Seven years, it took, from the roof of the doghouse to the lap of comfort.

The other evening, in the middle of some program, the people happened to look at the bed and see him there, brazenly and in full view, curled in a knot as small as possible for a dog his size, trying to resemble a cat.

"Do you see it?" one of the people said.

His near eye was slitted open, looking at them looking at him. Then the eye slid shut in satisfaction.

So far, he still eats dog food and does not join them for meals at the table. But time is his ally, and he takes the long view. There's no sure way of knowing how far patience may get him or where ambition ends. But it's a pity to see what's happened to him. The tough, utilitarian beast has become a lounging fop, whose taste now runs to electric blankets set on 6.

MAY

OVER THE YEARS, Rufus has inspired some strong emotions.

Appreciation, for one, when I see the diligence with which he goes about his work in the field. Anxiety, for another, when he used to escape the yard fence and I would have to careen, knuckles white on the steering wheel, wearing only pajamas, through neighborhood streets in some small hour of the night. Or rage, when in a moment of absent-mindedness or malice he would betray trust and defile a piece of furniture.

But one recent day I experienced a different and quite unexpected feeling. It was, I think, *pure envy*.

At the farm in a sweet time of the spring, with no work to do and quail out of season, we set out together after breakfast on an aimless ramble, without a particular destination or anything to hurry back for. By midday we must have covered six miles, maybe eight, through woods and glades, across streams, through clawing berry canes.

The sky was cloudless. Hardly a breeze was stirring. The cool of morning gave way to unseasonable heat.

Leg-weary, scratched and sweltering, I turned back more or less the way we'd come, and sat to rest awhile at a stream crossing before trudging the last

half-mile. My mouth was cottony. I was calculating what I'd give just then for a cold drink.

Rufus hove in view from some side excursion. He must have been tired, too, but you'd never have known it from watching him cover ground. Pure joy like that is what makes a walk without a dog a half-done thing. Straight down the woodland path he came, feet drumming, ears flopping. And without a second thought he hurled himself full into the creek—which was, at that exact instant, what I longed above all other things to do, but couldn't of course, being a human in clothes and shoes.

Immersed, with just his back and head showing, he drank noisily from the water that ran down clear over the pebbled bottom.

I licked my own lips, and worked my dry mouth, and almost could *taste* the coolness. But, being human, I had to wonder whose cows might be upstream in the next pasture—when what I really wanted was to fling myself face downward at the edge and quench a bottomless thirst.

He misses no meals. He devours the miles on legs that never fail. He enjoys his work—prefers it to any other thing. He bathes when it pleases him, and drinks what he likes without any bad effects. And afterward he sleeps until he wakes. And has no creditors.

If you hear of any higher state of happiness than that, please let me know.

AUGUST

THE SQUIRREL, a splendid athlete, vaults from the neighbor's tree limb to the roof of our garage, then hangs a moment from the eave by his hind feet, positioning himself to drop onto the three-quarter-inch-wide top of the wooden fence.

It never occurs to him that he might err.

Rufus is watching from the window well, like a missile in its silo, poised for launch. Only his golden eyes show over the uppermost rim of bricks.

The squirrel waltzes along the fence top to the bird feeder, lowers himself, selects a seed. He looks down into the window well at the dog, who imagines himself hidden.

The squirrel cannot understand how a creature that large can be so stupid. Rufus cannot understand how the squirrel can be so accomplished.

This has been going on for years.

Sometimes, to put a little adventure in his day, the squirrel descends from the bird feeder directly onto the ground. It is unnecessary bravado. He does it, I think, for the same reason some people climb sheer cliffs without a safety rope. He wants to experience life on the edge.

Rufus, in his hole beside the house, trembles violently. His teeth chatter—on a summer day, with the window open, you can hear it.

He has two choices. He can stay there, watching the squirrel play the deliberate fool at a range of about six feet. Or he can play the fool himself— make a futile rush, chase the beast across the yard and up the walnut tree, and have the empty satisfaction of having cleansed the property of squirrels for at least five or 10 minutes. Then the smug aerialist, that one or another, will come back to taunt and humiliate him again.

I can't remember ever wanting anything as much as Rufus wants to catch the squirrel. At night, when he yelps and twitches in his sleep, I'm sure that's what he's dreaming about. But even in dreams, where there's no limit on the possible, the squirrel must reach the tree first.

I was thinking the other day how that's a little like a writing life. Or maybe *any* life. You have a notion of what you want to do. It looks reasonable. So day after day, time after time, you come rushing out of your hole. And every time you fall just a little short.

Once I knew a wonderfully gifted man, an essayist, who confessed toward the last that he believed he'd somehow wasted his talent because he hadn't written a novel. Prose writers wish sometimes they were poets, needing to find only a half-dozen good lines a day instead of having to sell themselves by the pound. Poets humiliate themselves by trying to write plays.

The trick is in continuing to believe that anything is possible. And in that I take Rufus for an example. At the thing he was born to do, point quail, he's wonderfully accomplished. But it's the squirrel he wants. And, against the evidence, he remains utterly certain that one day the squirrel will stumble—or he'll learn to climb the tree.

He may be wrong, but faith like that is inspiring. And it lets him start every day with hope, as all of us must.

NOVEMBER

BEFORE HIS TIME in the White House ends, President-elect George Bush may have some things to apologize for. But, by heaven, his once-a-year quail hunt won't be one of them!

The animal-rights militants are outraged that a man elevated to the highest office in the land should have a fondness for blood sport. More and more, it seems, success in public life means knuckling under to every one-issue zealot who can print a sign, rent a bullhorn and collect a crowd of 10.

Anyway, in my experience quail hunting is not a bloody affair at all. It is a punishing walk, punctuated at long intervals by groups of startled men discharging their guns meaninglessly into the air, and disappointed dogs running to and fro on the faint chance there might be a bird to pick up.

While Bush was tromping the Texas brush country, I was out with friends nearer home. There were six of us—seven counting the farm friend whose land we hunted. We sallied forth at a civilized hour of middle morning into a freshly fallen snow, burdened with enough munitions to mount a successful revolution in some of the world's lesser republics. The day sparkled and was wonderful for bird-watching. We must have watched something on the order of 100 quail fly from under our feet across fields and over distant horizons. By accident, we injured a couple of them.

But we were happy, and our steps grew lighter as we walked. Furious shooting had relieved us of our cargo of shells. And the weight of two quail, distributed among seven hunters, is not onerous.

A few days after that our group held a wild-game dinner. It is not an annual event. Our last wild-game dinner, if I remember right, was five or six years ago. It takes that long to save up enough carrion to fill a platter, and some of it is pretty badly freezer-burned by the time it gets to the table.

Our wives are less than enthusiastic about these affairs. Quail jerky, like 200-year-old duck eggs, must be an acquired taste.

My contribution was a wild turkey that I shot some time ago, when I was younger, and had preserved in a cryogenic state like those artifacts people seal inside building cornerstones to be uncased and marveled at by later generations. In life the turkey had seemed very large. But the years somehow had diminished it.

"How many does it have to feed?" my wife asked.

"Sixteen," I told her.

"Sixteen people? *That*?"

"There'll be quail, too. We got another one this year."

"And ...?"

"And Leo has a honker."

"Beg pardon?"

"He has a goose."

"I see," said my wife. "And just out of curiosity, what do you suppose all this is costing?"

"Well, if you amortize the cost of the land, the vehicles, the fuel, the guns, the ammunition, the boots and clothes and special equipment like decoys and calls and whatnot—"

"And the dog."

"Right, the keep of the dog. Counting everything, we probably have something like $50,000 in it, maybe closer to $60,000. But it's a meaningless calculation. You can't put a price on pleasure."

"Divided by sixteen," she said, "that's $3,750 a plate—just to break even."

"Yes," I told her. "But just wait until you taste the 1982 potted merganser."

"What in the world is that?" she asked.

"It's a piece of history," I said.

DECEMBER

THE WEATHER HAD been foul, but then it moderated. Fred Kiewit called in the evening.

"Let's hunt the boys together," he said. "Rufus needs to get to know his son."

"Do you have a place in mind?"

"Anywhere. I'd just like to get them out before the year gets away."

"There's a farm I've hunted several times with a fine man—you might know him. Stuart Mitchelson. He's a lawyer in Mission."

"I know the name."

"I'll call Mitch and see if he can get away. Even if he can't, I don't think he'd mind us poaching on his territory. It's a couple of hours away, on the place of some good people named George and Mary Frank."

Mitch was tied up for that Saturday, and I could hear the regret in his voice.

"But call the Franks," he said. "I know they'll be glad to see you."

There'd been a hard freeze, with snow, and then a thaw. The harvested fields were slippery. After a little preliminary sniffing, Rufus and his boy set off about their work.

Rusty had grown into a fine dog—not quite as leggy as Rufus, or with as much white in his coat, but well marked and full of his father's desire. It was good seeing them together. And though we didn't find as many birds as Mitch and I had on our earlier outings there, we found plenty.

There was an especially grand half-hour in an upward slanting field of native grass. The large covey had flushed wild out of a brushy tangle at the bottom, without a shot fired, and had fanned out over the whole face of the hillside. We must have had a dozen points, first Rusty, then Rufe, always with the other backing.

"He's a wonderful dog," I told Fred as we slogged

back toward the car. "He has all of Rufus's spirit, and he may even have a slightly better nose."

"He's the best I ever had," said Fred. Rusty was his fourth or maybe his fifth Brit.

"I never thought I'd hear you say that, after Nixon."

"Nix was a great dog, and I cared the world for him. But Rusty's the very best."

What I felt then must have been something like a grandfather's pride.

SEVEN
1989

FEBRUARY

THINGS STRIKE YOU, sometimes, in a fresh and unexpected way.

The other evening I looked up from the pages of a book and noticed Rufus asleep on the rug beside me. And it seemed suddenly clear in that moment what a long way his tribe and mine must have traveled together—a longer road than either of us can ever know.

I don't intend to take chips in the everlasting argument between Darwin and the creationists, between science and faith. There's no profit in that, and anyway it's not essential to what I mean to speak of here.

What caught my notice as I looked at the dog—something veterinarians must take for granted, but which I'd never really considered before—was how remarkably alike the two of us are in our essential architecture.

Plainly stated, it stretches the imagination to think that random accident, nothing more, could have yielded so similar a set of solutions to nature's problems in constructing us. Whatever was the controlling force, and whatever name you choose to give it—whether natural selection or divine inspiration or something else—it seems obvious that more has been at work than just blind chance.

Nomenclature governs thought. Thus we speak of a

dog as four-legged. But the front appendages might as easily be called arms. The shoulders, elbows and wrists all operate exactly as ours do. The main difference is in the fingers—mine adapted for grasping and manipulating, his for walking on. The same with his true legs, which begin at a socketed hip, proceed down to a forward-thrusting knee and then to his ankle and finally a foot that, except for a bit greater length from heel to toe, is not so unlike yours or mine.

In the region of head and face the differences between us are largely cosmetic, and it's a matter of judgment as to who got the better deal. His ears are covered by fur flaps, which I would be glad to have on a raw morning. His nose projects farther forward and his dentition is different, but the general purposes of both are the same, smelling and chewing.

The greatest similarity is in the eyes, protected by lids with eyelashes. For both of us they're the principal means of receiving information about the world and, sometimes accidentally, giving back information about ourselves. His face, though contoured differently, is able to convey a considerable range of feelings: eagerness, regret, anxiety, amusement, fear, pain, anger and contentment. And to do it in a way that leaves no doubt about his meaning.

In the field, for instance, where we are equal partners, his expression is as businesslike as that of a

banker sniffing out false statements on a loan appli-
cation. And afterward, when the burs have to be
untangled from his coat, he lies quite still, knowing
that the ordeal, though uncomfortable, is necessary.

But the other evening, to document our alikeness,
I decided to make a few notes. First I flexed his knee
and foot, to verify exactly how they worked. He was
not pleased to be awakened for that, and glared up at
me with knitted brow.

When I came back with a measuring tape, intend-
ing to compare our dimensions from elbow to wrist,
he gave a little growl. There wasn't any threat in it.
Actually, it was only a peevish grumble, to let me
know there were limits to the fiddling around any
creature ought to have to put up with from another.

Even from a relative and friend.

JUNE

EVERY MAN'S BIRD DOG is a wonder—truly one of a
kind. I have not meant to boast too immoderate-
ly about mine. But Rufus's talents go beyond the
finding of quail. He is not so bad with marsupials,
either.

One night last week I let him out for his final tour
of the yard before retiring. He rarely lingers at that

hour. Like anyone of sense, it's bed he's thinking of. When I looked out a few minutes later, though, he wasn't waiting at the door. So I went to investigate.

Sure enough, he was on point. A very *stylish* point, if I do say so—nose thrust forward, stub of a tail extended, one paw raised, the classic pose you always see on hunting calendars.

The opossum also was on point, looking fixedly at the dog, nose twitching slightly, mouth open in a sharp-toothed grin. I have never attended any possum field trials, nor does the breed figure very prominently in calendar art. But to my eye the possum's point looked quite acceptable. Being nose-to-nose with a grinning opossum struck me as a bad plan, however, so I took Rufus by the collar and led him inside.

Then I went back out with a flashlight to have a better look. The creature still was there, still pointing more or less. I approached him gingerly, not wanting to provoke a charge. How he'd gotten over a 7-foot privacy fence and into my yard was a bit of a puzzle. The even greater mystery to me—and by now, I expect, to him as well—was why he wanted to be there in the first place.

But since he *was* there, I took the opportunity to look him over pretty carefully.

The usual place for observing possums is on country roads, where they tend to be about the thickness of a magazine, very still and generally unattractive. In life, however, they're not so bad to look at.

This one was a reasonably handsome beast, in fact. His snout was pointy, with a bright pink button nose at the end. Around the edges of his small ears there were some rather faint but attractive gray or brownish markings. In the flashlight's beam it was hard to tell the color exactly. And he seemed to have spirit. He wasn't playing dead, as possums are said to do—a reputation perhaps gotten from those flat ones on the road. This one held his ground, fixing me and my flashlight with a level if somewhat bedazzled stare.

It started me thinking, as we communed out there, how odd it is that some animals get all the luck and all the glory, sleeping on rugs in front of fires and having their pictures put up on walls, while some get none, and how for a possum as fine as that one there ought to be more to life than running under a tire.

I went on inside, then. But at the edge of sleep, with Rufus in his place beside the bed, I couldn't get it out of my mind. If a dog can learn to hunt quail, I was thinking, who's to say an opossum mightn't have a talent for it, too.

What a pleasure it would be to strike out across a frosty field, Rufus and the bird possum trotting together ahead, searching out the thickets. Let other hunters think what they liked. Their smirks would vanish when I came back with the game and they got none.

"Who trained him?" they would ask, with naked envy.

"Nobody did," I would reply. "He was a natural at it."

"Are you saying he points and retrieves? Everything?"

"That's right. He's the whole package. And this is his first season. By next year he'll be steady to wing and shot."

Just the idea of it got me so excited that I sprang from bed, went downstairs and got the flashlight from the drawer to have another look at him and see if he might care to spend the night with us indoors.

The yard was empty, though. The valuable bird possum had gone off to hang by his tail from the sign over some freeway, waiting for the morning rush hour. And I'd missed my chance.

NOVEMBER

THE QUAIL SEASON is well begun, and the bird population in our area this year looks to be abundant. What's more, Rufus, at 6 years old going on 7, is in his prime. For a dog as for a man, the threshold of middle-age is a good time for stocktaking.

Our outings together in the autumns of his first years were not so much hunts as noisy careens. He showed moments of brilliance. But more often his idea of a day well spent was to put a half-mile of woods between us and, once safely out of sight, to cleanse that sector of any birds that ever lived there.

I bought a whistle, thinking it might create some tenuous link of discipline, and blew the thing until I was purple in the face. He considered the whistle a fine idea. It announced my whereabouts, warning him when I might be about to come in view so that he could range more quickly ahead and re-establish his privacy.

It would have been something to watch those hunts from an airplane: a man with a whistle and useless shotgun, tootling and panting as he crashed through brambles and fell into sudden ravines, while a couple of fields away and over the next hill—as if engaged in some utterly unrelated activity—the man's dog would be seen chasing rabbits or rolling in offal or whatever else it is that such gifted and high-ly bred creatures do when no one is watching.

Rufus loved to hunt. I also loved to hunt. It would have been nice to have hunted a bit more often together. But that did not always happen. His early boyhood took me to the edge of spiritual collapse.

Maybe you have not raised a bird dog. Maybe you have raised children instead. Having tried both, I can testify the ordeal is essentially the same. Youth is glorious—provided it's *your own*. Youth in others usually is a trial and a torment. There are times when the most that can be hoped is that you all will pass through it without one of those eruptions of familial violence that make headlines in the newspaper.

There's nothing to do but wait the hard times out. Quail seasons came and went, and I began to notice Rufus's excursions in the world becoming less ambitious. Sometimes he actually appeared—just a momentary glimpse of dog against some far wood line—at a range visible with the naked eye. Once in a while, carelessly, he even let me overtake him.

I still recall that afternoon, about his fourth year I think it was, when I saw him locked on point along a fence. I tried to hurry to him, but the harvested field was greasy-slick with thawing. I remember how he turned his head to look over his shoulder at me slipping, stumbling.

"Would you mind getting a move on?" his expression said, clear as words. *"I've located some birds here, and I could use a little help."* It was his first acknowledgment that hunting might be in some way a collaborative enterprise between us. From that moment onward things have gone distinctly better.

The enthusiasm still burns, but under control—his control, not mine. Now when he tops a rise overlooking a patch of likely cover, it is clear that his mind is engaged. He hesitates an instant, considering the terrain. Then he goes about his work exactly as the hunter himself would, if the hunter were a dog. If the wind is blowing from an unfavorable quarter, he will make a wide detour to come back against the breeze, with the scent in his face.

We both sleep better after our hunts. What for a while was a contest of wills has turned into comradeship. It's wonderful to see the blooming of a fine intelligence, even if with a bird dog, as with children, that can take some serious waiting.

DECEMBER

OUR YEAR HAS ENDED with a hunt to remember. The day was mild for December, in the middle 40s with just a whisper of a wind from the west. My shooting friend, Patrick Dolan, and I stopped for early coffee and a visit at Bernard's breakfast table at the little north farm.

We'd been there twice before in the month, and rather than hunt the resident coveys again we decided to try Bernard's son's farm nearby. The corn had been harvested from the long field that ran from the draw below the house westward to the creek. Rufus made the long cast to the field's far end, then circled back, without finding any birds. So we went up the draw toward a place we rarely visited, with a pasture on the right and a weedy, sprout-grown meadow on the left, hearing several scattered quail flush ahead of us as we made our way through the trees.

Near the top, Rufus pointed in a little copse, and I stepped in behind and past him, thinking he'd found one of those wild-flushing singles. Instead, a huge covey—20 birds or more, an enormous bunch for so late in the year—came up all around me. Startled, I squeezed off one hasty shot, then marked where they flew.

They'd dropped into high grass farther up the hill,

along a raised bank with a fence atop it. Beyond the fence was a half-mile field of bare dirt, the crop litter plowed under. The birds had scattered out along the bank, and were holding tight, since that was the last of their cover.

What followed was the kind of dog work a quail hunter's dreams are made of.

Rufus would point. One of us would step in to flush the bird, and Rufus would slide under the bottom fence wire to retrieve from the open field. Then he would hunt a few yards farther on, point again, and the other hunter would put the bird to flight. We easily could have taken our limits from that one covey, if limits mattered.

Instead, we put four birds apiece in our game pockets, enough for both our tables. Then we called Rufus in and headed back down to the car. The hunter, if he means for there to be a next year, leaves half or more behind. Winter is long, and hard weather is the pitiless harvester of quail.

EIGHT
1990

FEBRUARY

FOR 10 YEARS, SINCE 1980, I have tried to persuade the Russians—in correspondence and in face-to-face meetings at their Washington embassy—to let me mount an expedition from the source to the mouth of the greatest of their Siberian rivers, the Lena. Born out of glacial melt in the mountains above Lake Baikal, the Lena flows more than 2,700 miles north to the Arctic coast, and has been closed to foreigners over much of its length since Stalin's time.

With the warming of relations under Mikhail Gorbachev the idea has gotten fresh life. And I am due in Washington tomorrow for discussions that could move the project toward a decision.

But sad news came today in a phone call from Stuart Mitchelson's longtime secretary, Renee. Mitch went in the hospital last week for heart surgery. He was nine hours on the operating table. Five bypasses were done. He'd seemed to get through it well and had begun to regain strength. Then, yesterday, one day before he was due to go home, a massive heart attack claimed him.

Lawyers hate leaving loose ends. His son, Tom, Mitch's partner in hunting and the law, would later tell me that his father a year before had made clear two specific wishes. One, that if his dear setter, Dolly, should follow him in death her ashes would be scattered on his grave. And, two, he would appreciate it if from time to time Tom would leave on his headstone the spent cartridge from an especially good shot.

It's too late to reschedule tomorrow's meeting with the Russians, so I will miss the funeral. But Mitch will be much in my thoughts. He was a devoted husband and father, a fine wing-shot and a lover of good dogs. I have many grand memories of our times together, but one particularly will be with me always.

It was the last point at the very end of a splendid day. The sun lay like a soft pink ball on the rim of a winter field, and man and dog were dark in silhouette against it as the bird came up. Rufus fetched it not to me, as he usually liked to do, but to Mitch. And, filled up with happiness, we went to the car, never suspecting that hunt would be our last together.

Men like that can't be replaced, but you are richer for having known them, and, even after they are gone, rich for being able to remember them.

APRIL

LIFE IS AN ENDLESS MIX of losses and new beginnings.

A friend has brought home a pup of a pointing breed. By his account it was a birthday present to his wife. But when anyone is thoughtless enough to mention that, the wife does not smile.

If you happen to be one who's committed to crisp days and the companionship of a dedicated dog, the time of starting with a young pup is wonderfully exciting. He may be clumsy and hard to live with at first, but the future is programmed in him. Hold a quail wing under his nose and already—at just 10 weeks or so—you can see his manner change.

If, however, you value domesticity and the companionship of a loving mate, it is better to concentrate on jewelry and candlelight dinners out and leave bird dogs pretty much alone. Lucky is the man who can have the best of both. I'm one of those. So was Mitch, my hunting partner of past seasons. And so, I hope, is this other friend I speak of. By profession he is an authority in conflict resolution, and in this crisis his skills should serve him well.

Certain things any owner of a hunting pup should know. Shoes and other articles of clothing *will* be eaten. Carpets *will* now and then be soiled—not with malice, exactly, but with a certain deliberate joy.

The outdoor doghouse, provided on the theory that a working animal prefers the bracing variety of the natural seasons, will prove unsatisfactory and in the end useless. It will be kept, like wedding pictures, as an artifact of one of life's moments of illusion. But the pup will choose a chair, and that thing outdoors will be forgotten.

Those are a few of the problem areas. But also there are benefits that the new pup's owner—the hunter's wife—might bear in mind.

From November through January, one-third of the calendar year, she will have neither the dog nor the man much underfoot around the house. The opportunities for weekend luncheons and the fellowship of her female friends—or *male* friends, for that matter—will greatly increase.

The freezer will fill up with the corpses of various small fowl. If a wife plays her cards right, insisting that he not only must cook what he's slain but also clean up his mess afterward, she will be the beneficiary of many delicious meals produced without effort on her part—elaborate dishes rich in protein, pinfeathers and lead pellets.

When the husband is traveling on business, he can be depended on to keep in touch more often by phone. He may have lost interest in the children, but he will burn to know if the pup has done anything new since yesterday.

I think it will work out all right for my friend. I know personally of men who have had five, six, a dozen bird dogs and who remain married to this day. Like anything else, it's a mix of drawbacks and advantages. It can turn out to be a powerful bonding experience. And if not, at least the lawyers don't have to argue over who gets the house and car and who gets the dog.

SEPTEMBER

RUFUS, WHO USED to escape whenever it suited him, and once even levitated over our 7-foot fence, has gotten a little thicker in the middle. Now he takes a lower view of life.

At the back of the yard, where the terrain is a bit uneven, there are occasional small spaces between the bottom of the boards and the ground. Several of these he has enlarged by patient digging—not for getting out, but just for looking through. For hours on end he'll lie motionless there, face thrust into the hole as far as the line of his brow. What he sees I can't imagine.

The main hole, the one he seems to prefer, affords

at most a limited aspect of the backside of the neighbor's garage on the next street. It's possible he can't even see the garage at all, although it's no more than a few feet away. Because in the no man's land between, there's a jungle of saplings and clawing vines that Hannibal himself couldn't lead an army through.

What is it that fascinates him so?

One dry day I got down on hands and knees and tried to look through to see for myself. But the aperture was too low, my head too large, my eyes wrongly placed. *Something* lives there though, that much is sure. Possibly it's the rabbit I've sometimes seen coming and going through that hole. Or maybe something else, some smooth-tailed thing I'd rather not know about, and wouldn't mention if I did.

Whatever it is, it goes about its secret errands in the wilderness behind the fence. And whether or not Rufus actually sees it, he knows it is there. His vigilance at the hole has intensified as the days begin to cool and the time of the hunt comes nearer.

He is a specialist—or used to be—bred for winged game, not furred. In past years I remember how he coursed the yard, nose lifted to the wind, hoping against the odds to catch a vagrant, fabulous scent of those feathered things that rise with such suddenness out of the autumn grass. He isn't doing that now, although I hope he will again when we're both clear of fences, with only a wood line and a frost-burned field ahead.

Until that day, which can't come soon enough for either of us, it's somehow sad to see him have to shove his nose between board and dirt and settle for the smell of any creeping, whiskered thing that happens to pass.

There'd be no loss quite as tragic as seeing him forget the true work he was born to. Dogs or men, time tries to do that to us all.

NOVEMBER

HUMILIATION IS A terrible thing to see, however it is packaged.

One day not long ago, with the start of the quail season at hand, I took my partner in for his annual trim. When a longhaired dog hunts the thickest cover—in with the stick-tights, briers and cockleburs—there's misery in the chase and an ordeal of maintenance afterward. So I wanted the loose hair gotten off his legs and ears and underside.

"Smooth him up a little," was how I put it to the groomer—one I hadn't used before. And later in the day I went back to claim him. Another hunter was in

the waiting room, and as it happened his pup, a female, also was a Brit. When she came of age, he said, he meant to get a litter from her, maybe two, before he had her neutered.

"Is that so?" I replied. "Well, have I got a stud dog for you!"

Hunters, being X-rated by nature, make propositions to perfect strangers that in almost any other context would offend decency and maybe even be punishable by law.

"He'll be up in a minute," I said.

The fellow waited, not wanting to miss seeing this powerful specimen of the breed. Soon footsteps and a scraping of toenails could be heard on the stair from below.

"Here he comes," I announced importantly.

The creature that appeared on the end of a leash was naked as a Chihuahua. Naked and small and cringing with shame. The man looked at him, then at me, then back at Rufus. Then he withdrew to his car without uttering a word. It pays not to say too much about another fellow's bird dog, especially when that other fellow might not be quite right in the head.

Rufus was so embarrassed that he developed a rash, and I had to take him to the veterinarian for treatment. It was a $45 rash. Then I had to get a special vest to protect his hairless chest and underside. That was $15. And that's not even counting the cost of the shave. I'd hire a lawyer and sue, but I already have so much in this that I can't afford the risk of losing.

They say it's how a dog works that counts, not how he looks. And that's true to a point. But I think it would take a lot of fun out of bird hunting to always have to be explaining what kind of dog you have and how he got that way.

It's my fault, and Rufus knows it. We're just going to have to get through this season the best we can. If we go after birds at all, it will have to be in some out-of-the-way place where people aren't generally met, in a field with plenty of bushes for me and the stud to hide behind if other hunters and their dogs do happen to pass by.

DECEMBER

ALL DAY HE'D HUNTED the high grass and the gullies, not once missing a stride or giving any signal of distress. And at the end of afternoon, when I called him in, he came grudgingly, not wanting it to end.

But when I unlatched his crate on the driveway to take him to the house, he was a pathetic sight. One eye was swollen entirely shut and mattering from under the lid. His right forefoot could bear no weight. And there was blood on the carpet in his crate.

Dan Hecker, our friend and veterinarian, has cared for him—and for all the creatures of our house-hold—from their earliest days. I reloaded Rufus and rushed to the clinic just before the closing hour. Dan had left for the day but his associate, Ward Brown, lifted Rufus onto the examining table.

"What's wrong, old guy?" he said.

It wasn't one thing, it was several.

"He has a small thorn in his cornea," said Ward. "I'll remove that. It may leave a little spot, but I don't think his vision will be affected. He also has a cut we need to stitch up." The cut was on his most delicate underparts. "Probably he got it going over a barbed-wire fence."

"What about the foot?"

"It's some kind of puncture wound. We'll have to see what's in there."

"I looked at it but I couldn't find anything. I feel awful."

"Don't," said Ward. "It went in between his toes. It's a hard place to see."

Any one of those injuries would have stopped me in my tracks. The amazement was how he'd worked the whole day, without once showing any distress.

"Dogs are like people," the veterinarian said. "They have different pain thresholds and his obviously is very high. But you see that a lot in bird dogs. As long as they're hunting, they forget to hurt. You'd better leave him with me. We'll have to put him under to do the repairs."

When I went back to claim him the next afternoon, Ward had something folded in a tissue.

"This is what I took from his foot. It was driven straight in but we got it all."

It was a hedge or locust thorn most of an inch long. I winced just to see it.

"Will he be all right?"

"You'll have to keep it medicated and change the bandage," said Ward. "In a couple of weeks he won't even know it happened. But I'd say his season's over."

NINE
1991

APRIL

LIFE BEING A CIRCULAR AFFAIR, it appears that we will once more be spending quite a lot of time visiting on the telephone with the Poison Control Center. The number used to be taped to the wall beside the phone desk in the kitchen. We'll have to put it up again.

Our daughters, in their early years, were omnivores. The medicines we kept locked inside a cabinet, but there was plenty of other stuff to eat. For salad there were the leaves of semi-toxic houseplants. When autumn added color to the menu, they were attracted to the fat orange berries of bittersweet. One of the girls would come smiling blissfully with crumbs of something horrid on her lips, and we would ring up our friends at the poison center to have another nice conversation about stomach pumps and ipecac.

The experts there are very thorough. They read from the literature as they speak to you on the phone. *How much of it did she eat? Are her pupils dilated? Is she alert? Is her speech affected?* Drastic measures never were required. Our girls were connoisseurs, tasting samples only. As soon as they were of an age to understand the meaning of a stomach pump and how one works, their grazing on the household vegetation ended. The hazard passed, and we took the number down.

The other morning, though, my wife was on the phone again. It was a strange and early hour, and I wondered whom she was calling.

"The veterinarian," she said. "But he doesn't know for sure. And the druggist isn't open yet. We'd better call Poison Control."

"You mean they're at it again?" I cried. The past flashed before me.

"No," she said. "Not the girls. I seem to have taken one of these." She handed me the bottle. It was Rufus's medicine, administered to prevent something with the awful name of heartworm.

"I got out a pill," she said. "And then I made a cup of tea. I was looking out the window at the sunlight and kind of dreaming. I started to drink my tea, and the pill was lying there and—well, I just popped it down without thinking."

I rang the number and a nurse answered.

"How old is the child?" she asked.

"It's not a child," I told her. "It's my wife."

There was a silence on the phone. "I don't think I heard you," the nurse said.

"You heard me. My wife just took the dog's pill." I was humiliated. Concerned, too, but mostly humiliated. There was another silence while the nurse turned the pages of a book.

"I can't find anything," she said. "I don't think this has ever happened before."

"Probably not."

"I'll put you through to a doctor," said the nurse. And in a second the doctor was on the line. "How much do they weigh?"

"Separately or in total?" I asked.

"Separately."

"One of them is about 100 or 105. The other's about 40 pounds."

"And your wife just took one tablet?"

"Right. She stopped herself at one."

"If you happen to have some ipecac around the house you might use that," the doctor said. "And I'd keep my eye on her for a rash or any trouble breathing. But I really don't think you have a problem."

"That's a relief," I said. "I hated to bother you, but I just wanted to be sure she wouldn't start barking or biting or something crazy like that."

"It's what we're here for," the doctor said.

I suppose now we'll have to begin watching for nips out of the houseplants and locking the medicine cabinet again. But it's nice to be reminded the service is there when we need it, and it's perfectly free.

MAY

Tᴵᴹᴱ ᶜᴼᴹᴾᴿᴱˢˢᴱˢ. In the first week of June we will leave for Siberia to begin the Lena expedition. Hundreds of loose details have to be attended to.

There's a ton and a half of equipment and supplies to be sent ahead by air container. Our medical chest, assembled by a doctor friend in Indiana, is on its way to us by express. New video equipment must be tested by our expedition videographer. Nearly every day there is a fax or phone call from our official partners at the Academy of Sciences in Moscow, with word of some new problem to be dealt with. The last of the funding from the expedition's sponsors is yet to be received.

Not the least of my worries is Rufus. He'll have to be kenneled again. It's only for three months this time, and not in hard weather. He's used to those lodgings now. The runs are spacious, the food is good, and he is known there. But it will be a lonely spell for him, and I can never leave him inside that pen without a little wrench of guilt.

"Don't worry," Fred Kiewit said. "Rusty's kenneled there, so I'll be going every day anyway."

"I'll feel better knowing you'll look in on him."

"They get along fine. I'll run Rufus and his boy together. Think of it as his little summer vacation."

That will make the leaving easier.

SEPTEMBER

WE HAVE TRAVELED the great river to its end. Returning from the Arctic, we were in Moscow during those dramatic days in August when the failed coup by hard-liners brought the final collapse of the Communist regime. We've come home to the comfort of real beds and something besides expedition rations, bringing with us 57 hours of video, 8,000 still photographs and 80,000 words of journal.

And now the hard writing begins.

Back when journalism was a noisy and less tidy craft, I depended on the racket of the newsroom to make the words come—the clatter of teletype machines, the dry rattle of manual typewriters, the shouts of *"Copy"* from reporters bawling for the services of a clerk.

We worked without privacy, all sitting in the open at desks strewn out across one vast, cluttered room. Of course, journalists were not so important then. All we did was tell the news twice a day. We had not yet taken on the reformation of society, the shaping of modern culture, the enforcement of political correctness and all the other burdens of intellectual philanthropy.

The raucous energy of the place was contagious. If for some reason I had to go to the office to try to work on a Sunday forenoon, the stillness was disabling. There is no place lonelier than a circus tent when the clowns are sleeping and the crowd has gone.

But everything changes. It is life's most dependable rule.

The machines of the newsroom are noiseless now. There's a carpet on the floor. The great room has been divided into a maze of cubicles, with padding to absorb any vagrant sound. The people who work there are more civil, generally less dissipated, more serious about their vocation. Certainly they are better dressed and less apt to return dysfunctional after lunch.

In this reformed and muted setting, the racket and the bawdy companionship are missing. So for the most part, now, I do my work at home. It has advantages. I can smoke when I want to, without risk of beating or prosecution. The refrigerator is close by. In the early mornings, when lady joggers of various ages and shapes go by on the street outside my window, I can make comments of a kind that, if uttered in the office, would get me hauled before a committee of my peers.

My only concern, with children grown and wife busy with her own affairs, was the danger of solitude. As it turns out, I worried unnecessarily. Rufus is with me.

As long as I am writing, he sleeps curled on a couch in front of the air conditioner. But when he hears the machine fall silent for a while, he comes to sit beside me and sometimes presses his nose against my elbow. His brow is knitted with anxiety. It troubles him, somehow, when I do not work.

I'm reminded, then, that if I don't keep on writing, neither he nor I, nor anyone else around here, will continue to eat. In which case we will not make it through to the start of quail season, which is 48 days away and counting. Just thinking about that brings back some of the old excitement of the time when the newsroom had wood floors and spittoons and writers were a hungry breed who lived on the margins. And one way or another, the words start coming again.

If a journalist is careful about the company he keeps, there's no better business in the world to be in. And Rufus is the best company I know.

NOVEMBER

THE DAY HAD BEEN perfection, despite a scarcity of birds. The cold morning had mellowed under brilliant sun. We'd hunted Bernard's son's farm an hour north—Rufus and I, Pat Dolan and Dolan's young German shorthair, Bo, a rangy, rawboned pup, still very much a learner.

We'd brought apples, cheese and part of a bottle of good claret, and loitered over lunch on the tailgate of Patrick's Jeep. Then we made one last half-mile circuit of the perimeter of the long field of corn stubble without result, and decided to call it finished.

The dogs were trotting indifferently ahead of us at the field's edge, only half-hunting. Suddenly Rufus made a hard left turn through the high weeds to the creek's edge, Bo following. It's 15 feet, at least, from the top of the bank to the water—sheer except for a narrow, grassy ledge partway down. When Pat and I fought our way through the weeds, that's where we found them, down on the ledge, Rufus pointing with his chin resting on a chunk of driftwood left there by some earlier flood. The pup, Bo, was rigid in place beside and a bit behind him.

There was no way down for a man. We scanned the grassy ledge, at most three feet wide and 20 long. No quail could be seen, and none ought to be in such a place. We tossed down sticks and lumps of dirt. No bird flushed. Then we tried to call the dogs back up to us, but they refused to move.

"One of us had better go down," I said. And I explored along the edge until I found a place where, by sliding and clinging to roots, I could descend. Moving gingerly to avoid a cold dunking in the creek, I made my way to where the dogs were still as statues, eyes fixed straight ahead.

"Nothing," I called up to Pat, stepping past the dogs and kicking in the long grass.

"No birds?"

"Nothing," I said. "Must have been a rabbit here."

Then the immense covey burst up, 25 or 30 birds, with that explosion of drumming wingbeats that almost stops the heart, even when you're expecting it. Unmolested by so much as one hasty shot, the quail stayed all in a bunch, following the course of the stream 100 yards back in the direction from which we'd come. Then they turned right together on cupped wings to settle on the opposite bank.

The dogs clawed and scrambled their way straight up from the ledge and were long gone by the time I finally regained the top. When we caught up, Bo was bounding back and forth at the water's edge. Rufus had swum the creek, 30 feet wide there. Dripping wet, he was pointing the covey on the other side.

The birds held tight again, and so did Rufus.

"Interesting problem," said Pat. "So what do we do now."

"I guess we wait."

And we did—10 minutes, maybe longer. Then the covey began to move. The birds were on open ground, and we could see them. So could the dog. He looked across to see why I wasn't coming. Surely, even for a man, such a fine bunch of quail was worth a wetting. Then Rufus took two quick steps after them, and the covey flushed again, straight away into a maze of saplings except for one nonconformist that wheeled out over the creek and fell to Patrick's shot.

Rufus had gone off after the main bunch, deaf to my calling. Bo, who'd seen the single fall, was whining in frustration. We looked at the bird afloat in the still water.

"He likes to fetch sticks," Pat said, and threw one out toward the bird. Bo swam out and retrieved—the stick. Next time it splashed a little closer. The feathered thing in the water caught his eye. Dog-paddling in place, he hesitated an instant while he decided between stick and bird. Then, making the right choice, he delivered the quail to hand and sprayed us liberally with his happy shaking.

The two of them motionless on the grassy ledge ... the point Rufus made on the creek's far side ... the pup's first water retrieve. Those are the snapshots that define a season and lodge forever in the album of a hunter's memory.

DECEMBER

I FEEL MYSELF YIELDING to a softness that I despise. Tomorrow there's a hunt. Another fellow and I are to go with our dogs to see if we can find a late covey or two. It will be cold, aching cold. Already it's the cold I'm thinking about, not the birds.

And that's strange, because I used to love a bitter morning—to rise shivering in the dark and pull on rough clothes, and be headed along some road at an hour when brittle stars still ruled the winter sky. I liked how the frigid air at first came seeping in like water through the heaviest coat. And how, after tromping through a covert or two, you forgot to notice that any more.

I found pleasure and a fine edge of excitement in winter camping, and once made a three-day walk alone across a stretch of timbered country, sleeping on the ground beside my fire at 7 degrees below zero, thinking I was in the lap of comfort when the temperature by midmorning had climbed all the way to 10 above.

A friend from years ago was in town for a visit recently. We were remembering a time we climbed a mountain ridge and lay down in our sleeping bags, wrapped in tarpaulins, and woke in the morning covered completely with snow except for the face-holes our breathing had made. It was true and had really happened. But, talking about it, there was the strange feeling that we must be speaking of something we'd only heard—something someone else had done.

As I write this, Rufus is napping on his couch in the room with me. I've told him about the plan for tomorrow, and he seemed pleased. He likes his comfort, too, but he's able to put that aside when the chance for working comes. That's the difference between us. I want my comfort *all the time.*

Anyone who's deteriorated that far has to find what pride he can in small things. For example, I awoke at a small hour the other night and wondered if there were burglars at the door or what else might have disturbed me. Then I realized my wife had her half of the electric blanket set on the highest number, 10. One year the controls somehow got switched under the bed, and we went a whole winter with her miserably cold and me thinking I was getting a relapse of malaria.

What woke me this time was only the radiant heat from her half, which almost had reached a meltdown. So I flung the covers off myself and moved as far from her as I could get without falling out of bed.

It's true our furnace is 70 years old and sometimes doesn't fire vigorously enough to send water to the upstairs radiators. In spite of that I've resisted becoming blanket-dependent. All right, *once* when the furnace quit completely and we were heatless for two days I switched it on. But only on 3, which is practically the lowest setting. And one other night when I was chilling with the flu. But apart from those two times, both excusable, my half of the blanket is almost as new as the day it came out of the box.

That may not sound like a lot to brag about. But each night the blanket sings its siren song, and I'm unmoved. As the softness claims me, it's the last frail proof of character I have left.

I will go on the hunt tomorrow, but only because it's the year's last chance, and only out of duty to the dog.

TEN
1992

MARCH

Among his other defects, he has a depraved appetite, preferring our food to his.

A sandwich left unattended on the kitchen counter, while the maker of it turns to get a soda from the refrigerator or gets called to the phone, is guaranteed to vanish in an instant. Our attention spans decrease as we age—though not his—and our reflexes are a heartbeat slower. So the loss of sandwiches is fairly regular.

Lately he has developed a lust for bagels. He will snatch them off the breakfast plate, from the refrigerator if the door is left briefly open, from a sack of groceries waiting to be put away. Even, sometimes, right from the hand of a careless eater.

On a recent day my wife and I had to make a drive of 100 miles or so on business. In a picnic basket—one of those with a lid—she packed some provisions for our outing. We'd gotten an hour down the road when Katie said, "I think I'll have a bagel. Would you like one?"

"Sure," I said. "I'll have a blueberry one." And she reached over the seat for the basket.

"That's strange," she said. "I don't find them. *You don't suppose ...*"

"Rufus?"

"He couldn't have," she said. "The basket was closed. But I know I put them in. At least I *think* I did. There were six of them in a plastic sack."

When we came home that evening, he was asleep in his chair. Under the dining room table was an empty plastic bag. We are not quick learners. And he is very skilled.

AUGUST

TIME IS SAVAGE. Live long enough, and the losses become almost more than you can carry.

Always for a dog, and sometimes for a man, the race is short. But to have had a desperate passion and followed it to the end of strength, to die unafraid, surely there is more than regret in that.

Fred Kiewit had two passions. One was for the work of newspapering, at which he was as accomplished as anyone I've ever known. He was what used to be called a rewrite man and was the dean of the paper's staff. When a story broke and the deadline was tight, Fred sat at the typewriter with the phone cradled between shoulder and ear, taking the calls from reporters at the scene. He wrote fast and wrote well. And from the jumble of facts and details pouring in to him, he shaped the story with faultless clarity in his mind and on the page.

He believed in his craft, and believed in anyone who practiced it fairly and honorably—even if he sometimes growled at them. To call in a story to Fred, then find that you'd failed to get some fact whose importance became clear when he asked the question, was to receive a lesson worth a year or two of journalism school.

His other passion was for bird dogs, Brittanys especially, and for the places you follow them and the people you follow them with, and for that time of year when the light changes and the fields brown. We must have had, over the years, several dozen hunts together. He was a large man, a powerful man. Friends sometimes called him *Kodiak*, partly for his stature and partly for his temperament. He could cover ground until those with him begged for mercy.

His wife, Vera, told how it happened.

He'd been bothered by severe pain in his abdomen and had seen his doctor, then had gone back to his part-time night work on the copy desk— not because he needed it, but to keep his hand in. After several days the pain worsened again, and Vera took him to the hospital. His own physician was out of town, so he was seen by another doctor filling in.

The problem was in his head, that doctor said. He didn't need medical help. He needed a psychiatrist.

But psychiatry is not known to be effective in the treatment of a perforated bowel, and only days later Fred was dead of peritonitis.

Colleagues spoke at his funeral, but the eulogies were unsatisfying. It's queer how, at such moments, newspaper people lose the capacity for telling the truth. The bawdy legends from younger days—the occasional brawls, the carouses, his wars with editors—all the real things were left out. He almost seemed sweet in the telling, and of all the wonderful things he was, sweet was not among them. But maybe that's how funerals must be.

I asked Vera after the service what would become of Rusty. Fred's son would take him, she said, although the son himself had been through one surgery for a malignant brain tumor and his own future was uncertain. I knew how Fred had worried about that. And though he'd died unnecessarily and too soon, some part of me was glad he was spared the grief of outliving either his much-loved boy or his life's best dog.

NOVEMBER

THE SUBJECTS I write about in my column general-ly are inoffensive, so most of the mail from read-ers is friendly. Once in a while a letter brings a scold-ing, and usually it's deserved.

Then out of nowhere comes a whoop of crystal-pure lunacy. Ones like that are rare, but they're worth the wait. The other day, shortly after Bill Clinton's election to the presidency, I got a gem from an animal-rights zealot who signed herself only Ms. Sue. Her communique, written in orange crayon on the stationery of a motel somewhere out in Kansas, I pass on here in its entirety.

> *We Democrats are in complete control of the country*
> *at last. We are going to pass laws that will stop you*
> *hunters from killing and raping animals. And we are*
> *going to take your guns away. Give it up. You can't*
> *win. Murdering of animals is going to stop.*

I'd have written her right back, thanking her for her interest and suggesting she take a subscription to *Field & Stream*. But the letter didn't have a return address. The ones from wackos seldom do.

What I would like to have asked Ms. Sue is just which Democrats she thinks are in control. I don't screen the politics of every bloody-handed fellow I spend time with in the field, but my suspicion is that a fair number of them are Democrats. They're at least as much in charge as Ms. Sue is. And what's more, they're armed.

For another thing, the new president-elect of the United States is famous for his inability to pass up a cheeseburger. Right now, in the feed lots of America, nervous steers are wondering not what the country will do for them but what they might be asked to do for the country. For if the leader of the republic, the biggest Democrat of them all, is calling for burgers, that implies someone is going to have to make a fatal contribution.

Finally, I wish I knew what Ms. Sue means when she talks about me and my kind killing and *raping* animals. Either she has lost her marbles completely or she has taken flight on the wings of metaphor.

Because while I have slain many creatures and hope to slay a great many more, the charge of rape is one for which I and my friends do not have to stand still—especially as we are primarily quail hunters. Anyone who would accuse a fellow Democrat, or even a Republican, of raping a quail must be speaking of a subject she has too much on her mind.

Letters like Ms. Sue's are fun to receive. But along with the giggles there always is a cold little undernote of dread, because you never know to what lengths the fanatically unhinged might go to make their point.

I can imagine a scenario in which Ms. Sue might creep out in a dark hour of a raw morning and conceal herself in a thicket where a covey of birds was roosting. And some time later I would pass that way on one of my search-and-destroy patrols.

Rufus would point the thicket. The covey would burst forth. And a fraction of a second too late—at the exact instant of firing—I would see Ms. Sue bound up from her cold nest, her beady eyes looking at me in a fury straight over the blazing end of the gun barrel.

And that would be a truly awful moment for us both. Because, however much she may disapprove of it, my hunting is governed by one ironclad ethic.

Anything I kill, I eat.

DECEMBER

I KNOW PRECISELY when, if not exactly how, it happened. It was a mid-December hunt, with the ground iron-hard and some patches of crusty snow. We'd toured the edges of a couple of favorite fields without finding any birds, and were crossing a fence to head back toward the car.

"Pass the dog on over," I told my friend.

But by unhappy chance Rufus landed sideways in an awkward way on the uneven, icy field. He gave a little cry, and I remember the look of surprise that flashed across his face. That likely was the first of the hurt. If I'd leashed him then, or maybe brought the car around to load him there, the outcome might have been different. But he gave no sign of lameness or distress.

At age 9, Rufus has reached that point in a bird dog's life when he has some sense. But he's not flawless, any more than is the man who follows him. I've eaten a few rabbits in my time. And Rufus has chased a few. It's a vice he yields to especially on days when quail are scarce. I wouldn't mind that so much—the Brittany, after all, having been originally a multipurpose dog. What's humiliating is how he bellows like a beagle while doing it.

Anyhow, as we started together up toward the farmhouse, a cottontail darted out of the weeds almost underfoot and raced down across a pasture toward a pond, Rufus in clamorous pursuit. The two of them disappeared behind the pond dam, where I knew there was a steep-sided ditch.

What happened there I can't say. But I waited a few minutes, then started down the hillside myself and met my partner coming back, pulling his useless right hind leg behind. That was the end of our day, and possibly of our year.

Now, after a week, the soreness seems less. But he still is unable to put much weight on it. I will try him a few days more on buffered aspirin, to see if it might only be something that will mend with rest.

In a year of hurts and losses, there's been another. Cinnamon, the old dog, is gone. We were composed about it beforehand, Katie and I, and understood the kindness we owed her at the end. But to know the right thing is easy. Actually to *do it* is immeasurably harder.

But then it all came back, unspoiled. How she had mothered so many cats and lived to grieve for some of them. How there never was a footfall on the walk that she did not announce. How she'd borne the coming of the new pup, Rufus, and taught him some civility. How, on trips to the farm, her first errand always was to race down the wooded lane to swim among the reeds of the pond, to which, in different form, she'll be returned.

That's how we'll see her, because memory is truer than anything time can do. She was a friend who came to us from the street, and she was 20.

ELEVEN
1993

JANUARY

I T'S THE INJURY every football player fears—a blown knee ligament, which means reconstructive surgery and then an off-season spent in rehabilitation. Some make it all the way back, some don't, depending a lot on will and temperament. It's hard enough if you're on a professional contract, with coaches and the press hanging on the news of your recovery. But it's an even lonelier business if you're a dog.

Our friends at the Hecker Clinic, Dan and Ward, examined him together.

The knee was loose, they said. It might recover a little more, and in the excitement of hunting—great as his tolerance for pain seemed to be—it was possible he'd ignore the hurt. But without the support of that ligament, the anterior cruciate, the cartilage soon would wear away and he'd be permanently arthritic.

Dogs hunt on three legs, of course. A really dedicated dog would hunt on one leg if he could find a way to do it. Rufus is an athlete, though. I could see him as he'd always been, devouring the distance like a bird in flight. To have to watch him go about it lamed and cautious, even if he found the birds, would be as sad as watching Bo Jackson hobble from home plate to first base on his prosthesis.

"My recommendation would be to go in and repair

the knee," Dan said. "Ward would do the surgery. He's the orthopedist and he's done a lot of them."

"What kind of success?"

"Very good," said Ward. "On a dog Rufus's size, about an 85 to 100 percent recovery of function. Not as good for very large animals. But a lot will depend on you afterward—keeping his activity restricted at first, then exercising the leg manually to keep the tone and range of movement. And finally building him back up gradually."

"How long will he be an invalid?"

"With any luck he should be hunting by next fall."

Dan and Ward are men whose judgment and skills we trust absolutely.

"Then I say let's do it," I told them, though I dreaded the further pain he would have to endure.

It was the right decision. On opening the knee, Ward found that the ligament—the one most important in giving stability to the joint—had not just been torn but had been ruptured completely, with only a few fibers still attached. There was no chance it could have gotten better.

The useless tissue was removed and replaced with sterilized monofilament, 60 pound test, drawn tight to snug the knee as nature's equipment had done. A day later the wounded warrior came home, and the patience-trying journey began.

FEBRUARY

FIRST IT WAS THREE weeks of a rigid bandage, then another week of a soft one. The wrap is off now. The hair is starting to grow back, so that his leg looks less like a freezer-burned turkey drumstick. And he's into rehabilitation. Actually, we both are.

We began with half-block excursions on a leash, with stops along the way to sniff trees and detect the passage of other tourists or convalescents. I do not bother to sniff the trees. I let him tell me.

The distance has been gradually increased. To a full block. Then two. And progress is uneven. Some days we come back sore and require an aspirin apiece—Rufus for his leg, I for the shoulder he's yanked out of its socket by lunging at the end of the lead. Week by week, though, I can see the gains.

By summer I expect we'll be measuring our walks not by blocks but by counties covered. He'll have gotten back a knee. I'll have lost 30 pounds of pies and ice cream and gotten back the shape I remember only from old photographs. People we meet along our route will no longer see a funny little man and his gimpy dog. We'll both be prancing champions of our breed.

"Here they come!" the other walkers will cry, falling back in admiration to let us thunder past. *"Just look at those two magnificent brutes!"*

MAY

WE MET THE COLVILLES, Sam and Peni, during our year in France. The publisher had given them our number there, and they telephoned to say that they would be coming to Paris with their children in a couple of weeks, but that their hotel reservations had somehow fallen through.

Paris in the middle of summer churns with mobs of tourists and several major expositions. The hotels, even the humblest ones, get booked full. To arrive in that city in June or July without a decent place to bed the family is a crisis of some importance. I know, because it happened to me once.

After some frantic scouting I was lucky to find lodgings for them, a small but congenial hotel in the Bastille area. It was only a little favor, but the beginning of a good friendship.

Sam and Peni have a Brittany named Abigail. In the days immediately after Rufus's surgery, Abigail sent him a cordial little note—written with help, I believe—inviting him to come for a swim at her lake when his mended knee allowed. Rufus replied, also with help, that pride wouldn't let him show himself with that naked drumstick of a leg. But he'd be pleased to come when he was decently covered.

The visit this week was a grand success. Abigail is

a beauty, so much like Rufus in expressiveness and marking that they could be littermates. They ran the lakeshore together and swam at the edge. Rufus spied a flock of Canada geese resting in the middle and was halfway out to them before our frantic shouting brought him back.

Motherhood was not in Abby's future. Spaying had seen to that.

"I can't help thinking, though, what a wonderful set of pups those two would have made," I told Sam.

"I know," he said. "I almost wish ..." He didn't finish, or need to.

JUNE

DAN, THE VETERINARIAN, came the other week for his annual inspection of our gang, and he was pleased with Rufus's progress. He shone a light into the pupils of those amber eyes and said he could detect the first faint shadow of cataracts coming.

"He's lost maybe 20 percent," Dan said. "But he'll see well enough for several years. Anyway, for a dog like him it's the nose that matters most. Something else will stop him first."

It was said casually. But it got me thinking. Rufus is 10, though nothing in his general look or his spirit shows it. In the cool of morning when we go out to exercise, I watch him running and it's as if no years had passed. There's no sign at all of a limp, though some days he stiffens a little after resting.

A great bird dog is like fine wine, always improving with age and more cherished as you draw the bottle down. We used to hurry the seasons forward. Now we try to hold them back—spinning out the time as carefully as we can. I'd guess that we have two more autumns in the field together. And after that?

Well, after that there'll be the couch in the room where I work. And his rug on the floor beside our bed. But I'm thinking seriously now that I'd like for him to have a pup to raise—a pup of his own, to keep the line going, on the chance the class of one generation can be transmitted to the next.

It's a nebulous quality, *class*. It can't be feigned, and it can't be learned. It's that quality a gifted actor has to command the stage before a word is spoken. It is a certain presence born of pride and undeflectable purpose. And although impossible exactly to account for, it is powerfully attractive when seen in any creature, two-legged or four.

I've gone so far as to locate the phone number of the man who owned his sire. I haven't yet caught the gentleman in, but I'll keep ringing until I get him, to see if he still keeps a Brittany or two and we might work something out.

What Rufus knows about hunting quail he learned mostly on his own, with only a little meddling by me. But the new pup would have an expert at his side—a veteran who on a remembered December day found and set 18 coveys of birds between frosty daybreak and the end of shooting light.

To see the two of them, Rufus and his pup, side by side on point at the wood line beyond a saffron meadow, would mean, for me, that those yesterdays could never be lost and the future was secure.

SEPTEMBER

THE MINNESOTA DAY began blustery and cold, with a suggestion of autumn in it. Squalls rushed in from the north over the shoreline of pines, whipping the lake to a chop. The one early-morning fisherman gave in to it, his motor humming as he fled the weather.

Then, in an hour, the storm blew through. The last broken clouds trailed away to the south, and the day was fine—the temperature mild, the air emptied of humidity and fresh as new wine. There is nothing quite like the sparkle of the north country on such a day, just on the cusp of the season's changing.

Rufus seized the moment for another swim. At home, in the swelter of midsummer, he let couch and carpet claim him. But here he has been renewed. He has ridden more car miles in a week than in all the rest of his life combined. He has been slipped into *No Pets Allowed* motels under cover of darkness, and has honored this trust by neither barking nor committing any other offenses.

It is his first away-from-home holiday, and he means to make the most of it. He runs like a pup on his repaired knee. He has explored thoroughly the lakeshore, the bordering woodlands and a nearby meadow. To keep in practice he has pointed toads, pointed squirrels in trees, pointed the hole under the cabin foundation where the skunk lives. One night he pointed the strobe lights on a distant radio tower blinking through the screen of trees.

His greatest pleasure, though, is the lake itself. He takes a wake-up morning swim. Then shakes himself and lies awhile to dry on the doorstep. Presently he goes to visit a swamp he's located somewhere in the woods and comes back deliciously fouled with black muck. This gives an excellent excuse for another plunge in the lake to cleanse himself. Starting at the boat dock, he makes a great half-circle out into open water, beyond the lily pads and back again—

paddling joyfully, nipping drinks of water as he goes.

I doubt that he suspects we are transients here. Probably he thinks we have come to stay, and that the days will turn forever to this sweet rhythm. He would like that. But the truth is, it's finished already.

Tonight, with the air gone October-crisp again, we stood out in the dark all together—the stars bright enough to touch, the Milky Way distinct as a footpath across the sky. We hoped there might be some remnant of the recent meteor shower, but it was over. Three falling stars were all we saw, and with the sky so vast and open here you can see that many any night.

Behind the trees and above them, there was a pulsing brightness that beat like a great, slow heart, then sent up protean bursts of white energy shifting and undulating overhead. Rarely do you see the Northern Lights so well. Rufus seemed not to notice. He'd gone off to see if the toad was in its crevice under the butane tank. Already, I suppose, he was planning his morning swim.

But there'll be none. It's over. Tomorrow there'll be only the cramp of the car and the long road. And after that the couch and the carpet, where he'll have to wait for the coolness to follow us south and let the true autumn begin.

OCTOBER

IN PUPPYHOOD HE WAS indifferent to storms. But over the years he learned his terror of thunder from old Cinnamon, who, at a rumble so distant it was inaudible to us, would scramble under the bed and quake in fathomless dread.

The other evening we went out for dinner. The skies were clear and we left Rufus in his yard. But while we were away a sudden, noisy little fall storm blew through and on. And when we came home we found him in a lamentable fix. He'd flung himself through the outer screen door and was caught, in an awkward position, between it and the inner glass one.

When we freed him he was limping badly.

"It's his knee again," I groaned. I could imagine the repair undone and another season lost.

"Are you sure?" my wife said. "Wasn't it his right one that was fixed? It's the left one he's favoring." And she was right.

Dan examined him at the clinic, flexing the knee that was tender and, while he was at it, testing the repaired one, which he found snug and strong.

"He may have strained the ligament," he said, "but I don't think it's a tear. We'll give him a shot of cortisone and see how he gets along." Older dogs, like older men, heal slower. But the soreness gradually decreased. He's sound again, now, and we've resumed our regular routine of early exercise together.

In the morning society of the park, everyone met is a friend. Fear may empty the place at night. But at an early hour, with the sun just risen, mist drifting among the trees and the dew-wet grass glistening, no thugs are abroad.

That's where we're training for the season ahead, Rufus and I—the same park where he went for his first puppy romps with Maggie. Come the first of November, it will be no use having birds in the thickets if our legs won't carry us to them. So, against whatever odds, we intend to arrive at that day fit as Olympians.

Our route is fixed. We leave the car under a big walnut tree on the park's west side, pass down through a swale and up to a hill crowned with oaks. From there Rufus can see the rose garden with its fountain pool in the distance. At that point I more or less lose control. He races on ahead, pausing from time to time to publish an advertisement of his passing. And by the time I reach the fountain, he's already in it.

Often, especially on Saturdays, there's a wedding in the rose garden. Sometimes there are several— one union following on the heels of another. I try to get there before the marrying starts, so that Rufus, when he finishes his swim, won't join the ceremony and shake himself all over the loving couple and their guests.

Usually, then, I sit on one of the benches. He sits beside me smelling wet-doggish. We watch the exercise walkers go past, their faces stern, doing funny things with their elbows. Jays come to water at the fountain's edge. Sometimes we see a chipmunk struggling with a walnut, a prize too big to get his jaws around, hurrying to lay up provender for the harder time he senses just around summer's corner.

The return to the car tends to be the social hour. We've run the foolishness out of us by then, and other dogs of the neighborhood are coming to exercise their people. The law holds that the people must be kept leashed, but the dogs in the morning park do not observe the rule. Most humans lead poorly on a cord. They are slow afoot and complain when a little yanking dislocates their elbows.

From a dog's perspective it is much better just to go your own way, turn your people loose and trust them to behave themselves. So, as we retrace our route, we generally meet several groups of our fellow creatures. Rufus races out ahead to convey a greeting, and I follow after. The pleasantries of sniffing and handshakes are observed. Compliments are exchanged all around.

There's a fine sense of fellowship, and nothing at

all to fear. Early morning people are unarmed. Morning dogs in the park never bite.

For now, these civil excursions are enough. But they are only preparation. As we drove home the other morning, Rufus sitting straight beside me on the car seat, I could see his gaze was fixed on some wider horizon than the one visible through the glass. The light is shortening. The air is changing. As autumn nears, his heart is ruled—as mine is—by the memory of russet wild-grass meadows, tan crop fields, plum thickets, tangled fence rows and icy brooks.

One day fairly soon the morning car ride will end not at the park but at the groomer's, his regular one this time, to have the year's feathering—the badge of idleness—shorn away. And he'll know then, beyond any question, that it's almost time.

DECEMBER

WE'VE BEEN TWICE to Bernard's place an hour north, and three times to our farm—to the grown-up fence row between two fields where there's always a covey in the berry canes and plum sprouts, dependable as a railroader's watch. They've been fine hunts, but short. I haven't wanted to test that repaired knee too severely in its first season.

The other day a friend had in mind a more ambitious outing. So, while I hated to do it, I decided to
let Rufus sit that one out. His resentment must have
been very great.

"I'm afraid I have some bad news," my wife said
when I came home. "The dog ate your company gift
certificate."

"Say what?"

"I was going to the store and had my grocery
coupons laid out. The gift certificate was with them.
He ate them all."

"Well," I told her, "there went our Christmas."

I have heard of companies whose employees
receive large holiday bonuses, but the whole idea of
gift-giving is a novel one for newspapers.

When I was a young man, new in this racket,
delivery people came jostling like ambassadors from
the Orient, bearing gifts for the top editors and big
shots in the business office. Boxes of chocolates,
crates of Florida grapefruit, cases of bourbon—nothing was too good for the men who could give your
product a friendly mention or put your daughter's
engagement announcement in a better place on the
page.

These offerings were not to be construed as tribute, but rather as unalloyed gestures of friendship
and good will.

We underlings, on the other hand, being by nature more corruptible, were forbidden to accept gifts of any kind or value. What we got instead—and were mighty pleased to have it—was permission to leave the office a couple of hours early on Christmas Day, so that we could arrive at the family dinner before the gravy had entirely congealed.

Just wait, we told ourselves. *Our turn will come!* But by the time we'd been around long enough to qualify for such perks, a new atmosphere of righteousness had pervaded journalism. An ethics code was written, ending the bonanza just when we'd managed to shoulder our way to the trough.

So what we all receive now, the mighty and humble alike, is a grocery coupon, exchangeable for merchandise at cooperating stores. I'm not complaining, understand. But these coupons have two large drawbacks. For one thing, like food stamps, they cannot be redeemed for cash. They must be used for the purchase of candy bars, Twinkies, nacho chips and other solid items of nourishment. What's more, as we have discovered, the certificates are subject to being eaten by the family dog.

"What will you do?" my wife asked.

"Do?" I said. "I can't do anything. It's finished, that's all."

Rufus said nothing—just smiled.

"Couldn't you ask them for another one?"

"Are you kidding? Go hat in hand, with some crazy story, like Bob Cratchit begging for a replacement goose. I won't do it! I have some pride."

"I'll bet they'd give it to you."

"Listen, I know these people," I told her. "They did not get where they are by giving double coupons. They are not men who lie awake at night, listening for the ghost of Christmases past."

"Well, it wouldn't hurt to ask," said my wife.

So in the end, putting my family's well-being ahead of pride, I did ask, in a thin voice, like a man expecting laughter or a blow.

"Heh heh," I said. "You'll never believe what happened."

They were very decent about it, actually. A replacement coupon was issued on the spot, and we had a Christmas after all.

"God bless us every one," we sang out together as we sat around the table.

"Bless the newspaper," cried my daughters, trying to govern their emotions. "And also the cooperating merchants."

Let it be said ever afterward that we journalists know how to keep Christmas as well as anyone alive, even if ethical scruples have somewhat diminished our seasonal opportunities.

TWELVE
1 9 9 4

JANUARY

THE SWOLLEN PRIDE of grandparenthood can be tedious, I know. So when the time comes, I must try to control myself and not bore everyone I know with vain gushings. This has nothing to do with my daughters, understand. They still are occupied full time with the perfection of their minds. It's Rufus whose longer future is about to be ensured.

The prospective mate has been located, although not yet actually met. Examination has shown Rufus to be free of any ailments and admirably fit—in spite of his age and his unbecoming devotion to the couch—for the duty that will be expected of him. The encounter likely will take place in February. Given the canine gestation period of just over 60 days and another eight weeks to weaning, it means that sometime in June the new pup will join our household, and Rufus, at just past 11 years, will have a son to raise.

I write that number almost with disbelief, wondering where the years have gone. In the brevity of their careers, the creatures we keep remind us of time's rush.

When he came, a wriggling package of energy and duck-fuzz, the children still were preteens in their rooms at home. They're young women now, voices on the phone and sometime-visitors from school.

I'm not handy with a camera, so the pictures I have are instants caught in memory.

Of his earliest puppy hunts, when it was clear already that luck had given me the dog of a lifetime. Of a point he made one winter day just as he was crawling under the bottom wire of a fence—frozen in that awkward posture, head turned sharply to the side, eyes fixed on a snow-covered tuft of grass.

Those of us who run with bird dogs and give them our hearts can be as tiresome as any grandparent. Suffice that there are a hundred other such moments, saved fresh as yesterday. And the background to those is a more general picture: of him in his prime at 5 or 6, scent-driven and tireless, a splash of orange and white flying effortlessly as a hawk along the dark line of forest at a pasture's edge.

We'll hunt again, maybe this weekend or the next, but more sedately, as suits our ages, measuring out the chase in easy hours instead of miles. Then the pup will come. We three will wait another autumn together, and I know already what sort of dog he'll be.

And if two of us are not as fleet, I hope we'll have the grace to watch without envy as he races on ahead, because what else is immortality about?

MARCH

HIS ELECTRIC DAY arrived at last—the day that would guarantee the continuation of his line. The breeder called from the kennel, in a pretty piece of country about an hour away.

"It's time," he said. "Bring Rufus on down." So, giddy as two youngsters off to the prom, we piled in the car and drove there.

How to speak about this tastefully? Let's just say it didn't go as planned. The first bad moment was when I got him out of the car, and one member of a group of hunters, there to watch the training of their pups, said, "Why don't you *feed* that dog?"

It's true, Rufus has gotten a trifle portly. So I had to explain about the game knee, the surgery. Missing nearly a whole season will cause anyone to take on a pound or two, especially when you've gotten to a certain age. Believe me, I know.

That little embarrassment disposed of, we went down the row of sheltered runs to meet the bride. Holly was the lady's name—splendidly pedigreed and about as winsome a Brittany as you'd ever hope to see.

"I'll put Rufus in the run next to hers so they can get acquainted a day or two," Jim Lyons, the breeder, said. And I drove home light-hearted in the expectation of a new grandpup. That was on a Saturday. Jim telephoned in midweek.

Rufus and Holly had spent some time together, he said. And Rufus liked her. He liked her a lot, in fact. Regrettably, however, his affection seemed to be … platonic. His idea of romance was to lie down next to her and wag his tail, with no clue about what else, if anything, might be appropriate.

His one previous chance to sire a litter was when he was not yet 3. Granted, nine years is a long time between. But I'd always thought, as they say about riding a bicycle, that it's a skill that wouldn't slip the mind. It occurred to me maybe he was self-conscious about his age. Or his waistline. Or was uneasy in those strange surroundings. Maybe he just *respected* her too much. Whatever the reason, his attentions were of a restrained and brotherly nature.

So I raced back down the road and brought them both home to Rufus's own turf, to see what might happen here. What happened is that he gave her a tour of the yard—showed her his doghouse, his water pan, the excavations he's begun under the redwood fence.

Then, when night came and I put Holly in a dog crate in the kitchen, he refused to come upstairs to his accustomed place beside the bed. Instead, he preferred to lie down beside her crate on the kitchen floor, nose between his paws, the very picture of domestic contentment.

Their next trip together, the following morning, was to the clinic of a specialist where—praise be to modern reproductive technology—it was arranged for there to be a Rufus-Holly litter after all. Rufus doesn't understand that sometime in early summer there'll be a new pup in the house, flesh of his flesh. For now, after taking a hopeful turn or two around the yard, all he knows is that his sweetheart is gone. He'll forget, though, because memory is short.

Everything in life being a metaphor for something else, I went straight out to the garage, then, thinking I'd better find out if I still remembered how to ride a bicycle. I located the old bike, all right.

And wouldn't you know it, the tires were flat.

APRIL

SAM COLVILLE HAD SAID he would like to get Abigail afield sometime with Rufus—not really to hunt, but just to see whether she might have an interest in the birds. I gave him a last-season's quail wing to tease her with, and a cap pistol to accustom her to noise. The wing game was all right, he reported. But she loathed the snap of the gun.

Picking a coolish spring morning we drove out—
Sam and Peni, Katie and I—to a game preserve, and
had the operator seed a field with a dozen quail.
Playful Abigail enjoyed the chance to frolic. Rufus
was pleased to see her again. But when I uncased the
gun and his thoughts turned to business, Abby was
content to watch him work, keeping a careful distance from the shooting. A dog not hunted young is
apt never quite to get the idea of it—though that's a
shortcoming of no importance in a family member.

Of the 12 birds, Rufus found and solidly pointed
eight. And all eight I shot on the rise, without a miss.
Neither of us really is that good. But, then, they were
pen-raised birds—not as explosive in flight as the
wild ones. And I think that both of us, rising to the
occasion, were showing off a little for our audience.

MAY

HOLLY HAS DELIVERED her pups, a splendid litter
of 10, and we drove to the country yesterday to
see them. Half are male, half female. Half have their
mother's coloring, and half their father's.

The pick of the bunch is mine, as fee for the sire's
service. A hunting friend in Florida and another in
Kansas both want Rufus pups. The one in Florida has

asked us to do the choosing. Holly looked on with some concern as Jim Lyons took them from her, carried them all together in a bucket, and put them on the grass.

They're hardly more than little worms, squeaking and wriggling blindly, eyes not yet open. Except for some rough idea of their marking, little can be told. It will be a month, at least, before anything of their size and personalities can begin to be known. I will be leaving next week for a month in France, to write a series of stories around the 50th anniversary of the Allied landing on the Normandy coast. Meantime, it will be up to my Katie and our daughters, both home now from college, to observe the transformation from worms into actual dogs, and to begin to detect some differences among them.

I do notice that several have their father's blaze of white from the crowns of their heads down over their stubby muzzles. But there's also a winning little fellow, plump, with a band of liver around his middle like a Hampshire piglet. The choosing, I can see, will be hard.

Tomorrow a man will come to measure for a new back door to replace the one that Rufus has destroyed over the years. The nature of a pup being what it is, I'm sure there'll be other replacement doors in our future.

SEPTEMBER

THE PUP, SINGULAR, turned out to be a plural. And Rufus has taken well to his new responsibilities.

His sons, Pete and Bear, are going on 5 months— no longer the foolish, yipping creatures of earlier summer. They are recognizable as Brittanys. And like me, I think, he can see the future in them. The genes of the parents seem to have passed intact. In appearance, Holly's Bear is the image of his mother, liver and white, with freckles. Pete, whose whole name is Rufus Repeater—that name a fervent hope—is orange and white.

They admire their father profoundly, as it seems to me any intelligent youngster ought to do. When he leaves his place on the couch in my work room and goes out to inspect the perimeter of the fence, they meet him at the door. He suffers the annoyance of their bounding up and nipping at his face and ears, and seems to understand it is a kind of tribute to his size and his position in the household.

Then, when that nonsense is finished, the happy *troika* tours the yard together.

We already have made several preliminary trips to fields and thickets where quail might be. The foliage still is too lush, its smell too overpowering for any serious work. But Rufus has shown them how a hunter must go boldly into the heaviest cover. And the necessity of returning, from time to time, to check on the whereabouts of their man, since men have but two legs and progress more slowly.

They've learned that riding in their crate in the back of the car can mean something good. They've learned the joy of coming home tired and sleeping with seeds matted in their hair. They've known the security of being praised for effort, and waking to a full bowl—rewards that every child, of every species, should be entitled to.

For now it's only exercise and an adventure. But there'll come a hard frost, and the meadow grass will pale. The weed stalks will dry and break, and the thickets will drop their leaves. And on one of our outings there'll come to the pups, powerful and clear, the scent remembered across a hundred generations of their line. Borne on the sharp breeze of a November morning, it will forever afterward rule their autumns and animate their summer dreams.

Even after all these years I remember how it was for Rufus—the way he halted in midstep, head turned to one side toward a weed clump, his expression a mix of astonishment and rapture. From that moment onward he was changed.

Pete and Bear have that still ahead. They have much to learn, and I'm depending on the seasoned veteran to help me teach them. He used to be what hunters call an all-day dog. That is, he'd devour the fields in a tireless gulp, resent the stop at the car for lunch, and still be plunging into briers and leaping ditches when the sun was getting low and the men who followed him had had enough.

He still has that desire, though the hunts are shorter now and over easier ground. And he's glad for an aspirin afterward to ease the aches. But there's a new bounce in his step this year as the season turns. He has these pups to get well-started, and for him— for both of us—it's a fresh beginning.

"You know," I said to one of my daughters the other day, "Rufus is like the brother I never had."

She considered that a moment.

"That would make him—what—*my uncle?*"

"I suppose it would."

"Then his pups are my cousins," she said.

"Right," I told her. "And you could do a whole lot worse."

NOVEMBER

SITTING UP STRAIGHT in the passenger seat, he watched the buildings go by, watched the traffic thinning. Then city gave way to suburban tracts, and finally to open country—undulating pastures, wood lots, the striped pattern of fields from which the crops had been taken.

I rested my hand on his back, behind the shoulders. And I could feel the trembling eagerness begin. He's going on 12 now. His boys, untested youngsters of 6 months, stayed behind in the fenced yard. Their turn will come. This first hunt of the season belonged to him.

We knew where the near covey would be, and it *was* there. From the house and barn lot the land falls away to the west, with a bristling hedgerow as a divider between two harvested fields. It rolled back the years to see him racing down the hill beside the hedge, his colors bright against the dark green of autumn grass at the field's edge. There was a time when he could cover ground that way for hours. But wisdom is a good trade for breakneck craziness. And what does it matter if the soreness comes tomorrow? A morning's hunt missed is one you'll never have again.

The covey was in the hedge, all right. But the

wind was wrong. The birds flushed wild, 15 or more of them, and planed down to the right—down into the overgrown draw below a dry pond.

I marked where they landed, all still closely bunched. And we went down there together. The quail would hold in that cover. It was a poor place for shooting, but the shooting didn't really matter. Rufus plunged into the weeds a stride or two. Then the scent of them came powerfully to him and he halted, eyes fixed ahead, muzzle thrust forward, like an arrow drawn and held.

"Easy, boy," I told him. And waited a moment until I was sure that perfect image had registered in my mind, then stepped in ahead of him.

They burst up around me in the thicket and were scattered and gone before I could see a one of them distinctly. We heard the racket of them rising, though, and caught brief glimpses of the small dun shapes ghosting off among the saplings.

There are three coveys on that place. The other two we never found. The morning warmed. A family of geese rode down the sky. We rested together in a sunny spot, then made the long walk back up across the field to the car. I wished there'd been one bird for him to find, hold gently and deliver. But except for that there's nothing I'd have changed. The autumn's new, and there'll be other days.

Sore-legged and swollen-eyed, he had to be helped up the stairs to his place beside the bed. Tomorrow the stiffness will be less. Another day or two and he'll be romping with the pups. And already he'll be thinking of open country again.

If we can help it, there'll be no rest for either of us until the hard weather comes. By then we'll have stored up good times to carry us through.

DECEMBER

T HE DAY WAS MELLOW, a bit too warm for this month. Away on every side rolled an infinitude of splendid country—harvested grainfields, old hedgerows, pieces of the original prairie.

It was very much like the country where Rufus began his career, and though he was just a pup there was no mistaking his willingness or his gift. I could imagine the seasons stretching ahead of us, although I couldn't know how dear a friend he'd be.

On that recent day, my hunting companion, George Alexitch, and I were together north of Manhattan, Kansas, with the papa and his two rowdy youngsters, Pete and Bear. They'd had that bit of work with a bird wing in the yard and had been out with Rufus on several of his conditioning runs in birdless country before the autumn turned. But this was their first real hunt, and I wasn't expecting much.

Their father goes about his work now in the way of a veteran, pacing himself, exploring the cover in a measured, sensible way. Sometimes Pete and Bear tagged along beside or behind him. More often they just romped, excited to be at large in a world unbounded by fences, assailed by scents they'd never met before.

Shortly before the lunch hour Rufus was pointing a covey in a thicket at the field's edge. As I came down toward him, I noticed off to the left, at the eye's corner, little Bear, still as a stone, honoring the old dog's point.

That, alone, would have made the outing a success. But there was more. It's a fine quail year in that country we were hunting. There were birds in abundance. One covey after another flushed through the hedgerows and out into the prairie grass. A situation like that can compress several seasons of learning into a single day.

By middle afternoon the two beginners were giving a fair imitation of seasoned hunters—searching out and pointing quail independently, honoring other dogs' points and finding downed birds. Anyone who's kept hunting dogs knows the luck of such a day. For anyone who hasn't, it's useless to explain.

The very last was the best.

We'd walked the whole afternoon into the breeze, and the day was nearly spent. The sun was low. It was that hour when you begin to feel the chill of evening through your coat. We turned back toward the car, the wind behind us, Rufus and I both gimping a bit—he on his rebuilt knee, I with the burden of too many years of doughnuts and other, worse dissolutions.

"Look at that," said my hunting partner, George.

In a grassy glade just ahead of us, the three dogs—the father and his two boys—were bent almost double, heads pointing back toward a thicket of brier they'd just passed. It was a fine tableau, the past and the future joined.

I wished, briefly, that I was carrying a camera. But a camera would not have done justice to the look on those three faces. Or to the great reach of country on every side. Or to all the other days and places that were recalled and made fresh in that instant.

So I photographed them with my eye, instead, and put the picture away in the place where days are always golden and good dogs and good friends are always young.

THIRTEEN
1995

JANUARY

IN THE HOLIDAY SEASON just ended, the house was filled with dancing, singing and eating.

The pups are the dancers. Pleased to discover creatures as fabulous as cats, they perform a comical little jig—looking over their shoulders and advancing rear-first, so the end that wags may be clearly seen. The tails are like a handshake offered.

But the cats, wanting nothing to do with either end, look down from radiator covers and countertops, singing their song of indignation and regret. All except the tricolored one, who won't be trifled with. She lurks under the upstairs bed. And when one of the pups strays in range, she rockets forth in a spitting, hissing display that, while harmless, is deeply impressive.

Equilibrium, I believe you could say, has not yet been established. The trick will be just to get through this next uneasy year or so.

Rufus is handling the trials of fatherhood about as well as could be expected. When they devil him too mercilessly, he expresses his anxiety in the same way many of us do. He eats.

One day my wife baked two pumpkin spice cakes and set them on a table in my workroom to cool before being iced. I stepped away from the typewriter momentarily, to make a cup of coffee or some-thing, and must not have gotten the door quite latched. When I came back, I noticed it was ajar and rushed in there with a shout. It was too late. Rufus already was face-deep in one of the cakes, crumbs of it clinging to his ears and brow.

Yesterday he ate part of a sack of powdered sugar that he pulled down from a pantry shelf. These little binges seem to steady his nerves and brace him for his necessary trips to the yard, where the lads are waiting.

For now they still are outdoor pups except at night, when they careen through the house a bit, then go to their crates in the kitchen for sleeping. So the singing of the cats is only intermittent. But hard weather has begun to set in, which means a full-time accommodation will have to be found. And I know that will happen. It always has.

In nearly 30 years, with several species of us under one roof, the only failure was with chameleons. The cats crouched at the terrarium glass, considering the problem. Then they learned to take the lid off, and our closed ecosystem instantly became a trifle less diverse. This time, however, the cats missed their chance. Pete and Bear have attained a size that makes eating them an unworkable solution.

And Rufus, for all his faults, would not dream of

devouring his young when cakes are available.

So we're a family, for better or worse.

FEBRUARY

FOR BIRD DOGS and the men who follow them, this is a cheerless time of year. The shotguns have been cleaned and stored. Boots still crusted with the mud of the season's last wet hunt are in the closet.

Before sunup on these cold mornings, when I go out to fetch the newspaper from the yard, Rufus waits just inside the door. But there's no eagerness, no crazy excitement, in his manner. Pajamas and bathrobe aren't a fit costume for the activity that rules his heart. He knows it's over, and the waiting has begun again.

Of the year's 365 days, only 92 are days of possible use. And of those few, we are lucky if we manage to spend 20 in the field. That's a narrow frame for a life. He can't do the precise calculation, of course, but he knows for a fact that many days get wasted.

He'll be 12 years old next month. Age and hurts have slowed him, as they do us all. But they haven't lessened his devotion to the thing he was born to do. I've seen people wear out, forget their purpose. But an old bird dog, when autumn comes, always can smell tomorrow on the wind. The question, in February, is how to pass the time until another November.

As I write this, Rufus is asleep on the couch three steps away, his head on a pillow. When his nose twitches and his eyelids flutter, I know that he is dreaming. Last night, lying on his side on the rug, he was running in full stride and yelping softly. I would have liked to have known exactly which moment of them all he was reliving. When I put my hand on his shoulder, he came back from wherever he was and looked surprised to find himself between walls, instead of in big country.

Memories are the capital that dogs and men have to draw on during these idle months. And the memories of the season past are very good.

There was that morning alone with Rufus on a familiar piece of ground, where the birds had coveyed in a place we knew they'd be and the sky was clamorous with geese and we had a world of sport, though not a shot was fired.

There was the fine hunt in rolling hills of crops and prairie grass—a day of so many quail that it was the start of the making of the pups.

There was a magical morning, when frost had turned the whole world white and furred every twig and fence wire, spent with a man who's made hunt-

ing and fishing his life, and who's as fine an out-
doorsman as ever shouldered a gun or cast a plug. He
is Harold Ensley, who, as The Sportsman's Friend,
was a pioneer of TV broadcasting about matters of
rod and gun, and whose syndicated program is seen
by millions around the country.

He had called in December to propose making a
film for his show featuring the veteran, Rufus, and his
just-started pups. Harold was a professional ball
player as a young man, and is an athlete still. It was
his first quail hunt since suffering a near-fatal heart
attack. With Dusty, his son, and Dusty's fine young
Brit, Covey, we must have gone six miles on foot,
maybe nearer eight. Harold never wanted to rest,
never missed a step, rarely missed a bird—was still
strong when the sun was low and Rufus and I were
ready for the car.

Finally, there was an end-of-season day with a man
I used to work with. The quail were wise and hard to
find, but we got our limit of conversation as we
walked, speaking the good names of people we'd
known together, Fred Kiewit and others, remembering our trade as it used to be.

Those are the saved times a dog and a hunter can
depend on. Like a film endlessly replayed, they'll
take us through until summer is past, the foliage colors again, and we can put our footprints in another

November field. And meantime, if like Rufus I run and yelp a little in my sleep, the woman I live with is good enough not to mention it.

MARCH

THE WEATHER OF THIS uncertain month is raw and foul. But it is a matter of no consequence to the pups, who have insinuated themselves and become household beasts.

First they were allowed indoors for brief periods to watch football games on television. I opposed it, believing that, the same as for soldiers and journalists, too much comfort can be the ruin of a working dog. But I was overruled.

I would not have gotten them beds. The ladies related to me did that. Now, instead of sleeping in their travel crates in the kitchen, they have joined us in the bedroom. I disapprove. The cats disapprove. Our opinions are worth nothing.

"They have a doghouse," I pointed out. "It's insulated. It's filled with hay."

Wife and daughters fixed me with unsympathetic stares.

"Doghouses are for summer," they said. "In winter, dogs come in."

"All right, have it your way. But you know what you're in for. They'll turn out just like their father."

"Rufus is a fine dog."

"Of course he is. That's not the point."

"What *is* the point, then?"

"You know perfectly well," I told them. "He sleeps on the couch. He pulls bagels off the counter. He eats whole cakes when no one's looking."

"So what's wrong with that?"

"What's *wrong* with it? For one thing, he is taking food out of my mouth. For another, it has destroyed his usefulness in the field. Before you spoiled him, his purpose in life was finding and pointing quail. Now he only points the refrigerator."

"The pups come in," they said. And it was settled.

Pete and Bear have not yet discovered bagels. Their taste runs to coarser things. They prefer wicker furniture. One of them will come prancing with an object in the corner of his mouth.

"What's that?" I cry.

"It's nothing," one of my women will say. "Just part of a chair."

Rufus, when he's caught at some offense, is able to convey the sense of great sorrow and self-loathing. But the capacity for guilt is absent in the young and must be learned. The pups, being without remorse, sin proudly, joyfully. If one article of booty is pried from their jaws, they go directly away to find another, having discovered that a house containing so many varied lives is infinitely rich in possibilities.

Patience will break them, though, as it does us all. It's odd the way a man takes up hunting, driven to satisfy something primal in himself. He acquires dogs and imagines the seasons ahead—imagines how they and he, nostrils filled with the scent of fur and feather, will prowl the woods' edge together.

But then the regulating hand of Woman is laid upon us. And instead of the half-wild, dangerous things we meant to be, we become house pets, poaching in the kitchen, sleeping on the couch. Our authority ended forever when we left the cave.

MAY

EACH MORNING I'm awakened by kisses of the moist and noisy kind.

No, I haven't slipped my leash and run off with some dance-hall floozy. These are *dog* kisses, delivered at that uncivil time when the sky outside the bedroom window has just begun to shade from black to gray, and when the only souls abroad are joggers, paper carriers and burglars headed home from their night's work.

The pups have decided that 5 a.m. is a splendid hour to start the day. Worse, with every week of spring's advance the dawn comes earlier. I tried to puzzle out what daylight-saving time will mean, but the calculation defeated me as it always does. I only know the interval between lying down and getting up is very short.

We have a routine.

They make their dash into the fenced yard. I get the paper from the walk and read it at the breakfast table until they present their faces at the door. Then we have our kibbles together. After that they go out again, and I go to my typewriter, and we all begin working at our holes.

Pete's hole in the center of the yard is his great accomplishment and pride. He can sit in it now with only his head and shoulders showing. The hole I've dug is even larger and has to do with banks and credit cards, a mortgage, the usual things.

Bear's diggings are more modest. He has created for himself a selection of little body-shaped nests in which to place himself for naps. Their house does not interest them. They prefer their holes, getting up from time to time to dispute the ownership of a stick, or, with much staring and growling, to play at being wolves.

But for the most part they sleep their days away, and there's the problem.

"What's the answer?" I asked my wife the other morning.

"I don't know," she said. "What's the question?"

She and Rufus had just come down at the normal hour for breakfast, and I'd already put in a full half-day.

"It can't go on this way. Look at them out there. Sleeping like babes."

"Yes," she said, "they're dogs. I don't think it can be prevented."

"But I'm wearing thin."

"Maybe they need more exercise. When you've been out hunting with them, sometimes they sleep clear through."

"Right," I said. "But the bird season doesn't come around again until November. I'll never make it."

"Then you'll just have to change your schedule."

"Change it how?"

"Write all night," she said, "and find a nice hole to sleep in during the day."

A man can keep bird dogs, or he can get a little sympathy. But he can't have both.

JUNE

IKE A HIPPO AWASH to his neck in the refreshing
waters of the Zambezi, the chocolate-and-white
one, Bear, peers out from his pool. Perplexed by such
behavior, Pete, the orange-and-white one, selects a
log from the woodpile and carries it off to the shade
of a bush.

Rufus observes these activities benignly from his
place on the patio step. For the moment they are not
pestering him—licking his face or nipping at his
legs—and parenthood is bearable. It is baffling to me
and perhaps to him how brothers from the same litter could be so unlike. And not just in color.

Rufus in his youth also was devoted to the water.
He would splash in his drinking pan until he emptied
it. So we got the kiddie wading pool. He would rush
across the yard and hurl himself into it with a flying
leap.

Then he outgrew that, moving on to larger
waters—ponds and rivers. So we threw the thing
away, but have had to get another one for Bear. Pete
wants no part of it. As far as he's concerned, the only
use for water is to slake a thirst. Bear occupies the
pool alone, wearing on his face that solemn, self-
important look men get while receiving a professional manicure.

He is the quiet one, a bit reserved. Whereas Pete is uncommonly vocal, having mastered a bizarre repertoire of yaps, yowls and whinnies. Pete also is strong-willed, as his father was. Hardheaded is another way to put it. Their differences in temperament will show clearly this autumn, their first adult season as hunters.

Bear will be the more tractable, the more careful. He will work closer and will look more often to fix the location of the man. Pete's legs will carry him in a rush wherever his nose leads. When called or whistled in, he'll be afflicted by a temporary deafness. That's how Rufe was at first—gifted, but barely governable. Then he was in the prime of his middle years, still with that splendid drive, but understanding everything.

They should make a fine pair, those brothers. One a plunger, a little reckless, charging headlong into thickets. The other a steady, dependable worker, tending to business, making certain nothing's missed. No two bird dogs are quite alike. You take the differences along with the talent, and value them for both.

For weeks Rufus showed no interest at all in Bear's pool. But now the oven of summer has heated up in earnest. The other day when he came in from his outing in the yard he was dripping wet from his tail to his collar, eyes shining, prancing like a pup.

That's how I feel, sometimes, when I see a basketball game on an outdoor court, or a bunch of boys playing touch football on the grass along the boulevard. The young may race by on stronger legs. But as they pass, they leave us an unexpected gift—the ability, across a reach of time and losses, to remember suddenly just how sweet it was.

AUGUST

WE'VE FLED THE midlands heat, again, for that spot beside the northern lake, where the days are mellow and the crisp night sky is dusted with frozen stars. Being there is splendid, but getting there can be an ordeal.

One daughter, working now in New York, arrived in Minneapolis on a midnight plane. The plan was to collect her at the airport, overnight in a motel, and drive on to the town of Blackduck the next day. But lodgings were a problem. The only vacancies were in palatial establishments, where the desk clerk's lip curled at the mention of a dog.

"Never mind," I said. "We'll find something outside the city."

We didn't, though. The hamlets are small, far

between and all but lightless. The old-fashioned mom-and-pop tourist cabins disappeared years ago. You'd as likely find a motel in the Gobi Desert as on that stretch of Interstate 35 north from the Twin Cities to Moose Lake. Time and the miles passed— much time. A man in an all-night gas station was not encouraging.

"I'd say Hinckley is your last chance," he told us. "It has an Indian casino. There must be rooms."

We got there at 20 minutes past 4 o'clock and discovered there'd been a Willie Nelson concert that night. People were sleeping in vans and under boat tarpaulins. There even was a man in a sleeping bag on the porch of the coin laundry. So we passed what was left of the night in a parking lot, Katie and one daughter in the front seat, the other daughter stretched on the back seat with Rufus, who did not complain that she used his flank for a pillow. I was on the floor between. Every half-hour a police car swung through the lot and an officer shone his flashlight in upon us.

I felt foolish and improvident. But now that we're installed in our cottage fronting the lake, it's just another funny memory of travel.

One day we went down a road through the pine forest to a clearing, where we picked a gallon of the wild raspberries that were coming ripe in abundance.

Once, as we made our way through the thickets, we heard Rufus give a strange, high scream, and I was afraid it was his leg. There was no lameness afterward, but that night we were disheartened to see he was behaving strangely—lurching a little to the side as he walked, sometimes falling, his breathing quick and shallow. He seemed restless and confused, pacing, unable to settle.

"I don't know what it is," I told the others. "It's possible he's had a stroke."

By morning the spell seemed to have passed. And he demanded to be let out again to explore his remembered lakeshore and swim happy half-circles from the boat dock out to the lily beds and back.

There's been one change. Since we've gotten home and I've gone back to the writing, I've noticed he rests less regularly on his couch. Sometimes he gathers himself but seems afraid to make the jump. Other times he bounds up to his place there, but then, as if he'd somehow lain in a cramped way, he emits that same strange, high screech we heard in the berry patch.

And giving up on the couch, he comes to sit close beside me, resting his chin on my knee as I type.

I have had him to Dan for an examination. There's no evidence of a new injury. If he had a stroke it was a mild one, for no aftereffects can be detected. It's clear, though, that whatever the episode was, it has cost him something.

OCTOBER

"I DON'T WANT TO UPSET YOU," said my wife, "but have you noticed the back yard lately?"

"Yes," I replied, "it looks like a cemetery-in-progress."

At that exact moment, Pete was peering out shoulder-deep from a new grave. And there were, of course, all the older holes, some his, some the work of his brother.

"What do we do?"

"There's nothing we *can* do," I told her. "We'll just have to wait for them to grow up."

"How long is that?"

"Who knows? It was years before Rufus had any sense, and he's 12 now."

"Yes," she said. "And yesterday he ate my purse."

"That's what I mean. It takes patience."

It is not good to be a creature bred for the open fields and the glory of the chase—and then spend endless months hemmed in by the tyranny of a fence. Nor is it easy to be a man whose joy it is to be afield with such creatures—but who must pass the greater part of the year anchored to a desk, face lighted by the sickly blue shine of a computer screen.

There's something about the leaves spinning down outside the window, the changing light, the freshness of the morning before the world's awake, that causes thoughts to stray, numbs the conscience and dulls loyalty to one's corporate masters half a continent away.

So we are counting the days, Rufus and his pups and I. Not quite a week remains until the quail season opens and we give in completely to our madness. Meantime, we make the time pass in our various ways.

Pete and Bear tunnel on toward China. Rufus lies on the rug beside me, regretting his excesses (the purse did not go down as well as he might have wished), hoping his gimpy legs will carry him to another covey or two. And I am typing steadily from the breakfast hour until dark, going at it like a man killing snakes, hoping to get written far enough ahead to cover my indiscretions.

"You shouldn't work so hard," my wife said.

"There's no help for it," I told her. "I have a heavy burden of irresponsibility to carry."

"How long is the season?" she asked.

I knew the answer by heart.

"Seventy-six days. Ninety-two if we finish January in the neighboring state."

"That's a lot of time to waste."

"It's not all wasted," I told her. "I'm allowing myself two days."

"You mean that's all you'll be hunting this year?"

"No. Two days to *write*. I can be fast when I have to be."

There was about her the sadness of someone who has bet the rent on a three-legged horse.

"When will you grow up?" she wanted to know.

"It takes time."

"How much time?"

"Who knows? Like I said, you just have to be patient."

After all, we haven't yet been married even 30 years.

NOVEMBER

HE WOKE IN DARKNESS and had his moment in the yard, then stationed himself inside the front door, keening softly. With eyesight dim and hearing all but gone, he would take no chance of being left behind. Not on this most important morning of all the mornings in the year.

I don't know what the signs were that told him it was the day. The gun had been put in the car while he slept. The boots were left in the closet until the final moment. And yet he *knew*. Always, the evening before the day, Rufus has known.

It is the 13th autumn of our time together, and I would not have dreamed of slipping out without him. It does not matter that his hunt this time must be short. Old dogs still have the glory in them. Old dogs cannot be left alone to grieve.

In some areas, I'm told, other men's outings were spoiled by a downpour. But the weather at our place was fine for it—cool, with just an occasional spit of rain in the air. And it seemed right that Rufus should have the field to himself. At least for the first hour of the first outing of the season that may well be his last afield.

There was no crazy careening, no foolishness. He spent his hour sensibly, pacing himself, going about it in the way old dogs do, hunting with his head instead of his legs—nose lifted, working deliberately into the breeze, letting it carry its messages to him.

When uneven ground or a malicious vine sent him sprawling, he would right himself, not humiliated, only vexed. And I pretended not to notice. I see him as he is, but also as he's been. And in memory's eye he still is young. I remember the first bird he found and fetched, and the look on his puppy face at that moment. If I tried, I believe I could remember each of the ones after, though there have been a great many. I can see the streak of him across a meadow, then on point at the far edge, waiting for me to arrive to do my part.

Every hunter should have such a dog at least once in a lifetime, and I have had Rufus, and by the miracle of things remembered will have him always.

On this day, in the hour allowed, two birds were staunchly pointed, found in the tangled weeds and delivered. Two only, but quite enough, since there is more ceremony than purpose in the first morning. He was ready then for the car seat and a nap.

He did not mind that it was the turn of his pups, Pete and Bear, who, loosed from their crates, set off immediately on a mindless adolescent frolic. They romped, explored, and after a while they worked a bit. But I'd not have a pup without some play in him. They'll steady soon enough. Too soon, because hardly has that happened before you have to begin counting down the years.

Time is quick. Quick for all of us, but quicker for these creatures that share our lives. And now, given the luck of another autumn, we'll be measuring out our season, Rufus and I, hour by precious hour.

DECEMBER

THE TWO LETTERS came only days apart. Both told of losses, but they had to do with more than that.

One letter told of a man who'd died while hunting with a friend during the opening week of the quail season of his 67th year. For the fraternity of us who keep dogs and cherish autumn days together, that is the golden time. The letter was from his son.

The two friends had found a covey in a hedgerow. The birds had scattered on the rise, and his father had gone alone back down the fence line to see if he might locate a single. After several minutes the friend missed him, followed in the direction he had gone and found him where he'd fallen—taken instantly, it appeared, by a heart attack.

"I know nobody wants to die," wrote the son. "But I know that Dad would have chosen this way to go."

The other letter concerned a man who was a year older, at 68, and who'd died just one day later, on the first day of the duck season.

"He was in his favorite blind with his golden retriever, Amos," wrote his wife of 44 years. The Friday before she'd gone with him to the lake, when he put out his spread of decoys in readiness for that opening morning.

If you've ever hunted wildfowl, you know how that morning would have been. The fine excitement of going out in darkness to your place. The near company of the eager dog, companion and partner. The first show of light coming low over the water. The rush of wings overhead just before the shooting hour.

The season had begun well. The three ducks he'd taken, and that Amos had retrieved, were with him in the blind. On his little two-way radio he had spoken with his friends in other blinds around the lake.

"Life can't be better," he'd just told them. Then more flights of ducks came slanting in over the decoys.

"Shoot!" they were calling to him over the radio. But he didn't answer.

When they got to the blind, the retriever, Amos, was so frantic they had to use a hunting coat to restrain him while they tried to help their friend. But it was no use. He was gone. His heart, like that other man's, had stopped.

The letters also told about the funerals, and about what people had said that was of comfort. They're somber affairs, funerals. Naturally there was sorrow—the letting go is hard. But there was more than grieving.

For those two men had lived fully to their last

breath, had raised their families, and had left life in exactly the way they would have wished. So there was another thing the mourners spoke about, and that was *luck*.

Hunters' luck.

Dan met us at the clinic after hours.

"When we went out for dinner he was fine— asleep on the rug, " I said. "An hour later, when we came home, he couldn't stand."

"Not at all?"

"He tried. He could almost get up and stumble a few steps. But he can't really walk. And he's in a lot of pain. He cries out when you pick him up."

"Well, let's have a look at you, old fellow."

Three weeks before, they'd drained and treated an abscess on a rear foot. He'd responded well to the antibiotics and was his usual cheerful self in only days. But the problem now was something different and larger.

"Appetite?" asked Dan.

"Good."

"And drinking?"

"Until this, everything was normal. What could have happened in an hour?"

"It's hard to say. It could be a systemic infection. Or an injury of some sort. Or possibly a tumor. We'll run some tests first thing in the morning and take some pictures. We'll know more then."

But the results of the blood work were in the normal range. And the X-rays revealed nothing. A dose of cortisone brightened his spirits, but the pain still was great. He'd given up even trying to stand. Daily I went to visit him, most days twice. And it was clear he was losing ground.

"He's stopped taking food, stopped drinking," Dan said. "We're hydrating him by IV. But here are the results of the blood tests we made this morning. He's beginning to lose some kidney function. It's not critical yet, but it's a bad sign. We've checked for everything we know, and frankly we just don't have an answer."

At Dan and Ward's suggestion, specialists were consulted. He was taken to a clinic where more tests could be done and where doctors were on duty around-the-clock. I spent time with him there, sitting on the floor beside his mat, hand on the sleek chestnut fur of his fine head—so much time I must have made myself a nuisance.

One evening Sam Colville brought Rufus's friend Abigail to the clinic for a visit, and that touched us both almost more than we could bear.

"I think we're losing him," I said to Sam.

We've had such griefs before. We'll have others. You'd think, with practice enough, you'd learn finally to compose yourself. So why did my shoulders shake so as I said it? And what was that sudden hotness on my face?

FOURTEEN
1996

JANUARY

TWELVE AUTUMNS WE traveled the fields together, and were prodigal with our time. Almost to the last we did not consider endings.

He flew the fences. I clambered ungainly over. He plunged boldly into the thickest, prickliest cover, while I took the easy way around the edges.

"The pup has *style*," a man once said, and I thought I'd won the lottery. He also had much courage, and a ruling passion. If I'd ever gone at writing with a dedication like that, there's no knowing what work I might have done.

"He'll live in his house outside," I told my wife when we brought him home. "He'll be a hunting machine." That lasted until the weather cooled. Then of course he joined us and the old dog and the cats indoors. He slept in a chair or beside the bed. But when we returned from an evening out and he met us at the door with that look of innocence, we knew there'd be a warm place on the covers where he'd trespassed. He could be devious. A sandwich unattended for a moment would vanish in a gulp. His lust for bagels was indecent.

But those were merely vices.

His abiding devotion was to the hunt. He marked the season's turning, and when the alarm sounded in the dark of a November morning, he always *knew*, and was waiting already beside the downstairs door.

His eyes, gold when he was young, deepened to chestnut brown. A knee failed and had to be repaired. He hunted on it eagerly as ever, not seeming to mind the price of soreness afterward. Then the cataracts began to come, but it was his nose that brought the important messages, and the nose still was keen.

Nearly every man who ever walked behind him spoke of someday wanting a Rufus pup, and several had them or have them now. One of those was Fred Kiewit, who, in the year when we were in Paris saw to it that the autumn was not wasted. Fred is gone, too, now. As is that other fine man, Stuart Mitchelson, for whom Rufus pointed and brought to hand the last bird just at the mellow sundown hour of the last day Mitch and I had together. All of them—those men and Rufus—had full lives, good lives. And good lives never are long enough. But in the end there are some things that medicine cannot fix.

He passed his last night at home, on a pallet in the kitchen, with me beside him. He was tired, and had borne enough, and had been too good a friend to hurt any longer.

In the morning, then, I dressed for the hunt—put

on my boots, and folded my canvas coat beside him, with the bird smell still in it. Also his leash. His head came up from the blanket. He'd have stood if he could. All the old excitement was in his eyes.

Dan, who'd cared for him so well from earliest puppy days, made the sad house call. Came to kneel with me beside him. And just as I let Rufus take the quail wing from my hand, released him to wherever it is that old gun dogs and those who've followed them finally go.

With my wife and a daughter I drove to the farm, and on a day of false spring, working together under a warm sun out of season, we buried him, wrapped in the coat, facing a thicket in which he almost always found a covey.

My theology is a bit shaky, and I don't profess to know what, if anything, lies beyond the darkness. But I believe in covering all the possibilities.

So before we walked away, I looked a long minute straight up into the cloudless deeps of that sweet springtime sky and said, in my heart if not actually aloud, *Freddy, Mitch, I'm sending you a pretty good dog. But he isn't given, only loaned.*

JULY

THE SWEATY FIST of summer holds us tight.

As I sit here at the typewriter, the pups are lying in the back yard, flat as if they'd been dropped from a plane. The heat has dulled Pete's interest in carrying logs. He prefers the slight coolness of a spot of bare earth in the shade of the walnut tree. Bear, after a dip in his pool, is air-drying.

I don't know if they miss their father. They seemed to need, or at least expect, more attention for a while after he left their lives. But they have the entertaining company of one another.

The routine of their days is invariable. In the early morning, just at first light before they're called in for breakfast, and again at the end of afternoon when the blaze of the sun has started to go out, they wrestle and play tug of war with much mock-growling. The middays are napped away, although usually with one eye slitted open to detect any squirrel incursions. At night they join the society of cats and people in the upstairs bedroom. When the light goes out, they prefer the place where Rufus used to sleep, on the floor at my side of the bed.

They're just past 2 years old, still youngsters in spirit but fully grown. There are times, as I watch Pete patrol the yard or notice his face at the glass of the back door, when I believe for a startled instant it's Rufus I'm seeing. But despite the power of that resemblance, I have no favorite between the two.

They are, in all likelihood, the last bird dogs I shall own. I intend for us to cover a lot of ground together. Fifty-some days remain until the equinox, when the planet will begin to tilt a little toward the dark. Waking sometimes at a small hour of morning I imagine that I can feel already another autumn coming.

There are not many things able to tempt a man, well on past middle age, to wish the seasons forward, to wish time away. But once more now, with Pete and Bear, I yearn ahead.

Courtesy of Talis Bergmanis

About the Author

C. W. GUSEWELLE has written for *The Kansas City Star* since 1955. He has written five other books, and in 1977, he received the *Paris Review*'s Aga Kahn Prize for Fiction. He and his wife have two daughters.